"*Atlas Girl* is more than a book; it's a journey in which Emily Wierenga takes you by the hand and invites you into the broken places in her life. She shares the unexpected beauty God has created in those places as he's made her heart whole again, and how he can do the same for you. If you've ever been hurt or gone through a hard time, this book will give you hope and a new understanding of God's love for you."

—**Holley Gerth**, bestselling author of *You're Already Amazing*

"The best memoirs combine the storytelling elements of a novel—smart pacing, tactile details, people you care about—with the deep insights and spiritual takeaway of great nonfiction. Emily Wierenga deftly serves up that rich blend in *Atlas Girl*, a nonlinear, wholly moving account of her life's journey so far. Her honesty is raw, real. Her faith is hard-won. And when it finally pours out, her love—oh, her love soars off the page and makes a nest in our hearts. Brilliant and beautiful."

—**Liz Curtis Higgs**, bestselling author of *Bad Girls of the Bible: And What We Can Learn from Them*

"This isn't just a book, this is a journey. Of grief and wonder, loss and gain. Emily tells a world-spanning story that this world needs in *Atlas Girl*!"

—**Jon Acuff**, *New York Times* bestselling author of *Start* and *Stuff Christians Like*

"Every journal chronicles a journey, and I'm glad to have traveled with Emily on hers. Reading this book isn't a diversion; it's an adventure. As you read, may you get lost and found, as I did, on your own road to home."

—**Jeff Goins**, author of *The In-Between*

"When I finished this book, I wanted to give Emily Wierenga a standing ovation for writing such a deeply personal memoir that

I literally could not put down. *Atlas Girl* is moving and beautiful and all heart."

—**Annie Downs**, author of *Let's All Be Brave*

"Emily opens wide and allows a beautiful and aching vulnerability in the words of *Atlas Girl*. It is a story of stories that gently shares of pain, of almost-lost faith, of what love does to a frail soul in a frail body, and how even in the twists and turns of life, *we make it*. If you could use some 'making it,' *Atlas Girl* will sit with you, offer a shoulder, and minister hope through story."

—**Sarah Mae**, author of *Desperate: Hope for the Mom Who Needs to Breathe*

"This is the kind of spiritual memoir I love. The story is vulnerable, insightful, and artfully told. You know you're in the hands of an expert writer—and yet you never feel like style is getting in the way of heart. I thoroughly enjoyed every word and didn't want it to end."

—**Heather Kopp**, author of the memoir *Sober Mercies*

"*Atlas Girl* is both a vulnerable memoir about the sacred art of learning to love and be loved and a gentle reminder to embrace being home, wherever you are."

—**Myquillyn Smith**, author of *The Nesting Place*

"Raw, emotive, and lovely . . . Emily Wierenga's memoir is captivating, descriptive in imagery and emotion, and you can't help but find yourself in her story. Emily's willingness to honestly wrestle through the disappointments and difficulties of life will give you courage to face your own."

—**Jenni Catron**, church leader; author of *Clout: Discover and Unleash Your God-Given Influence*

"I'm not sure if Emily Wierenga's *Atlas Girl* is poetry or prose, or just deserves its own category of lovely word crafting, but what I do know is that it is transporting. Her gifted weaving of time and place and story captivated me from the first page and held on to me as I floated, fully engaged, throughout the entire book. Emily said, 'We don't live for ourselves. We live for all of those whom our lives touch,' and her arms reach out and touch the life of the reader as she shares the intersection of people and God in her own life. Cheering, clapping, loving this book and the woman who has borne her soul amidst the pages."

—**Logan Lane Wolfram**, executive director and owner of Allume; author of *Life for Dessert*

"Emily's story captured me from the first page—she is an immensely gifted writer with a knack for taking her reader on a journey of experience. I felt like she was giving me an atlas of my own, asking me real, important questions about my own walk through life. Her story about loss, life, and love is worth its telling—I'm glad Emily's told it."

—**Tsh Oxenreider**, author of *Notes from a Blue Bike: The Art of Living Intentionally in a Chaotic World*

"*Atlas Girl* is both a journal and a journey; a trek of a woman who discovers heartache, happiness, and hope around the globe and a chronicle of the musings and meditations that accompany the blessed, bumpy ride. Emily's tender vulnerability and honest questions point you to the Lord who already knows the final destination. The best part? You will unearth bits of yourself as your tag along for the sacred voyage."

—**Karen Ehman**, Proverbs 31 national speaker; author of *LET. IT. GO.*, *Everyday Confetti*, and *A Life That Says Welcome*

"*Atlas Girl* is about the layers of life that matter: generations and caretaking and love and grief. It is here, tucked in these layers of Emily's stories and heartbreak, that Jesus is found. We see that to be a child, a grandchild, a parent, a spouse, a friend is to be a citizen of this world. And though our feet are planted here on earth, no matter our location or our circumstances, the kingdom of heaven is palpable and near. Travel with *Atlas Girl* as she unfolds the layers of her journey around the globe to the center of her heart."

—**Alexandra Kuykendall**, leader and mom content editor, MOPS International; author of *The Artist's Daughter: A Memoir*

"Emily Wierenga's *Atlas Girl* is a heartfelt reflection, poignantly told, of growing up in the shadows and light of ministry life. She spares no longing, sensuality, heartbreak, ambiguity, or epiphany in telling her story. I wish that all spiritual memoir coming from evangelical circles would be this true-to-voice, grounded, and real. Take and read—you'll be glad you did."

—**Mike Morrell**, journalist and party-thrower; mikemorrell.org, buzzseminar.com

"Not all critics agree, but I believe sometimes we read to find friends. Such is the case with Emily Wierenga's *Atlas Girl*. Her vulnerable prose wooed me right out of the blocks and held me to the very end. More than some Everyman, Emily is an Everyfriend. Her journey lays bare the painful grace we all must sooner or later shoulder; that no, the world is not perfect but yes, we can make it seem close for the people we love."

—**John Blase**, author of *Know When to Hold 'Em: The High Stakes Game of Fatherhood*

"Emily bravely takes us on a journey through this writing, courageously showing us the pain behind the pulpit that can exist. The transparent story shared about her pastoral family's life is sure to bring help and healing to many with silent frustrations."

—**Tara Jenkins**, EdD, Sr. pastor's wife, FellowshipChicago.com; founder, MinistryMates.org

ATLAS
GIRL

Other Books by

Emily T. Wierenga

Save My Children
The Story of a Father's Love

Chasing Silhouettes
How to Help a Loved One Battling an Eating Disorder

Mom in the Mirror
Body Image, Beauty, and Life after Pregnancy
(cowritten with Dena Cabrera)

A Promise in Pieces

ATLAS GIRL

FINDING HOME IN THE LAST PLACE I THOUGHT TO LOOK

EMILY T. WIERENGA

BakerBooks
a division of Baker Publishing Group
Grand Rapids, Michigan

Published by Baker Books
a division of Baker Publishing Group
P.O. Box 6287, Grand Rapids, MI 49516-6287
www.bakerbooks.com

Printed in the United States of America

Library of Congress Cataloging-in-Publication Data is on file at the Library of Congress, Washington, DC.

ISBN 978-0-8010-1656-1 (pbk.)

Published in association with MacGregor Literary Agency.

14 15 16 17 18 19 20 7 6 5 4 3 2 1

Dedicated to my husband, Trenton Nathan Wierenga—
our love is the greatest journey.

And to my mum, Yvonne Patricia Dow—
for teaching me how to dance.

That's life and faith too.

Messy,

blurred, and

beautiful.

And even as Dad lifted Nanny's limp body from the bathtub and Mum ran to her bedroom, even as the ashes sat on the piano while Allison played "How Great Thou Art," the lines were blurred. The picture was messy.

But it hung on the walls of our hearts, unfinished.

And it was **home**.

Contents

1

Mum

Canada: Blyth, Ontario

July 2007

> Behind all your stories is always your mother's story, because hers is where yours begins.
>
> Mitch Albom

The smell of my hands reminds me of Africa.

Of mangoes mashed, of Mum feeding me, and my brother too. And now I'm feeding her, and she doesn't open her mouth when I ask her to.

The sunrise sky is pretty, like Mum's pink silk scarf, the one hanging in her closet, and the windows are dirty; maybe I'll clean them today. Mum thinks today is Sunday—funny, because yesterday was Sunday too, she thought—"And there's church and I will need to take my blue purse with my Bible and where are my glasses?"

This is what she would normally say, but suddenly she can't speak. Kind of like me until age four because we moved so much, and Dad says I just watched people. Just stood at the fence in Congo and watched our neighbors.

Mum is trying to ask me something, but her mouth won't work. I busy myself with the spoon and the mashed fruit. I might as well be buying baby food for the way Mum can't chew. I don't have children of my own and this is something Trent, my husband, wants. "Maybe one day," I tell him.

I didn't used to want children at all, and now I'm bathing Mum, who's had brain cancer for five years, and I'm changing her and cutting her toenails and my womb is too full of grief and wonder to make room for a baby.

Funny how the two go together, grief and wonder, kind of like when Jesus died and his murderers realized he was God even as the sky tore.

The sky is bleeding red, and in a month it will blaze cerulean with late August heat. Combines whirring and the air thick with the meaty smell of harvest.

And Mum's still fumbling for words, and when she does talk she has a British accent, but now she has nothing and I wish, I wish she knew how much I loved her.

"Bigger," Mum says finally, and I know she's trying to say, "I love you bigger."

"I love you biggest," I tell her, wiping drool and mango from her chin with a cloth. It's not supposed to be this way.

I'm helping her stand now, and she's light. She hasn't been this small since Africa, where she knit afghans with local women while Dad taught blind men how to plant and Keith and I played in the mud, him in his cloth diaper and me in my underwear.

I read somewhere that stress can trigger brain tumors. Perhaps Mum's grew when she found Nanny in the bathtub, dead. Or maybe this tumor is my fault. Maybe it's from when I got anorexia, Mum holding me at night when she thought I was asleep, and her crying.

Or maybe it's from all of those pots and pans flying across the room when she and I would fight. Or maybe it's from when I left the house at eighteen and didn't look back.

Mum's diaper is poking out of her stretchy pants, the ones she always wears because they're the easiest to pull up if she's unconscious, and there's someone at the door and I'm helping her across the floor toward her blue recliner.

And Mum is asleep in her chair even before I answer the door.

2

Leaving Home

Canada: Edmonton, Alberta

September 1998

> The journey of a thousand miles begins with a single step.
>
> Lao Tzu

Mum had said to sit close to the bus driver, so I sat as far away as possible.

And now a Chippewa man in a red bandana with stubbly cheeks was snoring on my shoulder.

He smelled like communion wine, the kind my father served in glass cups that we slid, empty, into the pew's tiny cup holders.

He smelled like beer, like the late August summer when I was entering puberty, cleaning up the Corn Fest fairgrounds in my Sunday dress with my family. The beer cans all clanging like empty songs against each other in their black garbage bags. It was what good Christians did, cleaning up after sinners' parties and marching in pro-life rallies, and it was always us versus them. And all I ever wanted was to be them.

But always, we were taught to be kind to *them*, so I let this man sleep on my shoulder in the Greyhound bus headed west while I tucked up my legs and tried to shrink inside my eighteen-year-old frame.

I tried to close my eyes against the cold of the window but it had been two days since I'd hugged my younger brother, Keith, and my sisters, Allison and Meredith; since Mum—whose name is Yvonne, which means beautiful girl—had held me to her soft, clean, cotton shirt and her arms had said all of the words she'd never been able to voice. The Reverend Ernest Dow, or Dad, had loaded my cardboard boxes full of Value Village clothes onto the bus and kissed me on the cheek and smiled in a way that apologized. I was the eldest, and I was the first to leave. But then again, I'd left long before getting on that bus.

I'd slid my guitar, then, beside the cardboard boxes, its black case covered in hippie flower stickers and the address for the Greyhound depot in Edmonton, forty hours away.

And we still weren't there yet, and I hoped there would be mountains.

I should know, I thought. *I should know whether or not there will be mountains.*

My parents had raised us to believe in God, to believe in music, and to believe in travel.

We'd visited Edmonton as children, piled into our blue Plymouth Voyager, and we'd driven from Ontario to California, no air conditioning, living off crusty bun sandwiches and tenting every night.

And there was Disneyland and the ocean and me nearly drowning because I was all ribs, my body too tired to care. And we'd traveled home through Canada, through Edmonton, but all I remembered was the mall, West Edmonton Mall, and how it had hurt me to walk its miles, thin as I was.

I was hospitalized soon after that trip. The submarine sandwiches hadn't been enough to fill the cracks. But oh, how my parents taught us to love the open road. We caught the bug young, and here I was, and I couldn't remember where the Rockies began and ended.

I scratched at the night as though it were frost on my window, but all I could see were the bright yellow lines on the highway, like dashes in a sentence, like long pauses that never ended. The last sign had said Lloydminster, a town that stapled Saskatchewan and Alberta together.

And for some reason I always said a prayer for her when it was dark. *Mum.*

Not really during the day, but always when it was night and maybe because she was like a candle. We didn't talk much and we were opposite in temperament and so we yelled a lot, and yet I missed the way she smelled of lavender and would hold me when a boy dumped me or when Dad wouldn't listen to me.

The man with the alcoholic breath was whimpering in his sleep and I felt sorry for him, and annoyed, and I had a crick in my neck. No one seemed to notice this blonde girl with the man asleep on her shoulder, but that was the way I wanted it. No one seeing me, all hunched over with my Margaret Atwood novel and my Walkman.

I was listening to Journey. "Just a small town girl, livin' in a lonely world . . . she took a midnight train going anywhere . . ."

I closed my eyes against the jagged yellow of the road and buried my nose against my cardigan. It smelled of fuzzy peach perfume. Of the mission trip to Atlanta, Georgia, to the 1996 Olympic Games; of the twenty-one-year-old boy who had given me my sweet sixteen kiss.

It smelled like home and my room covered in Michael W. Smith and DC Talk posters and the floral quilt with Cuddles, my bear. And I didn't remember Dad ever entering that room. Mum sometimes slid books under the door, books on sex and why not to have it before marriage, and sometimes my sisters would come in and watch me do my makeup.

Ever since the anorexia—me starving myself from age nine to thirteen and ending up in a hospital where my hair fell out and my nails curled under—my sisters had been a bit scared of me and I didn't blame them. Mum didn't let them visit me very often because I played secular music from the radio, stuff like Bon Jovi and Bryan Adams, stuff that made the insides of my legs ache a little.

I twisted the silver purity ring on my ring finger and it wasn't coming off, not until my wedding day, and it was the one thing my parents and I agreed on.

But I would have pulled the Kleenex from my bra, and the bra from my body, for Seth Jones. For the scratchy way he said my name and the way his brown hair hung over his eyes, but I hadn't.

And Mum had knocked on my bedroom door that day, roses in her arms, and she'd sat on my bed and held me, the day Seth had dumped me in the school courtyard. The day he'd said I was too nice. Which really just meant I wouldn't get undressed for him.

But then Mum had given me the bouquet of roses and my fingers had bled from the thorns. And I'd known I wasn't too nice, just too afraid of sin, and sometimes it doesn't matter what kind of fear, so long as it steers you right.

I didn't know why I was waiting except that sex was a big deal, even bigger than drinking, and it was only allowed after marriage.

Not that marriage meant much with my dad sleeping on the couch after staying up late on the computer and Mum getting jealous over the ladies Dad talked to after church in his long minister's robe, his face full of laughter, a sight we rarely saw at home.

"Edmonton," the driver's weary voice crackled over the speaker, and the man on my shoulder was sitting up now, rubbing his eyes and yawning. As though he did that kind of thing all the time, as though we were lovers or friends, and I shrugged.

Stretched my legs. Tugged my green cardigan close, pulled the photos of my roommates from my cloth purse. Alex de Groot, short with dark curls and more of a smirk than a smile, and Meg

Hendriks, tall and Dutch and blonde. They would both be waiting for me, Alex had told me in an email.

The bus was stopping and the Chippewa man inched out of his seat.

And I stood up, and my heart fell out of my chest and I couldn't breathe.

For all of my eighteen years of not being able to connect with him, I missed him. My father.

I missed knowing he was there. That he could fix anything I asked him to.

That when he was at the wheel, I could just fall asleep in the backseat because Dad would get us wherever we needed to go.

That if I had a math problem I couldn't figure out, he would spend hours at the kitchen table showing me over and over how to do it.

And if there was a thunderstorm or a scary dream he would sit outside my room until I fell asleep, reading his book there on the floor by the light of the bathroom. Like a shepherd.

Dad was the one to teach us piano and the recorder. He played guitar but he knew the chords on a piano and we all sang and played instruments. There was a lot of music in our house.

I gripped the seat in front of me, braced against this sudden wave of homesickness.

We were stepping off the bus now and I saw my roommates standing there and they looked just like they did in the photo.

I wiped my eyes. Cleared my throat. And walked toward them.

We were sheep, waiting to be corralled, and there were forty of us.

Most of us were eighteen years old and fresh from home, our hair oiled and our faces squeaky clean and Scripture tucked under our arms because this was Bible school.

Mount Carmel Bible School. A square brick building on a plot of grass in the heart of Capilano, Edmonton, just blocks from the townhouse I shared with Alex and Meg who listened to the Canadian indie band Sloan, and lounged in the living room talking for hours, and cooked delicious suppers.

And there were no mountains.

"Gosh, this is lame," Alex said now, doing her smirk, and I loved her already. Loved her way of reading comic books in the bathroom and walking around the house in her bra and underwear like she didn't have a care.

We all huddled, silently checking each other out in the entrance of the school until a man with a long face and glasses ran in like he'd forgotten something and saw us.

"Come in!" He gestured. "No need to be shy! We're meeting in the conference room."

So we filed in, the sheep that we were, and I didn't see him.

The boy I would one day marry.

The boy who would hold me for nights on end while I shook from anorexia and insomnia.

The boy who would make my heart beat a thousand times faster for the way he smiles. The boy who would make me laugh, every day, for the rest of my life.

Maybe I didn't see him because I'd promised myself I wouldn't marry someone from Bible college (or "bridal college") because it was too cliché.

But I saw his friend.

A tall boy with a Greek nose and olive skin who caught my eye and winked, and I forced myself to turn away because a man up front was calling for our attention. His name was Victor Rendusso. He stood beside the guy with the long face and glasses, whose name we'd later learn was Darb Kelly—and Victor looked like a sergeant with his clipped moustache.

"Welcome to Mount Carmel, class of 1999," Victor said. "You may take your seats and we'll start with a few songs." And we did. We sang some church songs with a woman on the piano in steel-iron curls and it felt like summer camp.

"See any cuties?" Alex leaned in and I shook my head.

"Not really. Maybe that guy." I nodded my head at the Greek, across the aisle. "But he's probably a player. You?"

Her eyes went big. "Oh yes. To our right. The brown curls. He's mine."

His name was Patrick Stolte and he wouldn't be hers. She would go on one date with him, and end up marrying another boy named Lane Dougan, who was also there, who also had curls. A boy who was best friends with my future husband, Trenton Wierenga.

I wouldn't notice Trenton until our housewarming party one week later, the one Alex and Meg would throw and I would attend because it was in our house and I couldn't hide out in my room doing homework forever.

So I tiptoed around that night saying hi to everyone and pouring myself soda while the others drank beer and coolers and the Greek boy fell drunk down the stairs.

He'd already asked me to save myself for him—me, and a couple of other girls—because he'd promised some guy he wouldn't date for six months as a dare and so he was getting all of the girls he was interested in to promise the same. And we fell for it, for him and his wink—that is, until he fell down drunk, and then I saw him.

Trenton. The boy from the farm, the army-boy who got down and did a break-dance move in the middle of the living room floor. As I watched him dancing on the floor, it all caught in the back of my throat, all of those love songs and the loneliness, it caught like a big wad of gum. He was tall and strong with a dark brown crew cut and large hazel eyes.

It would be years until we finally got married. And we'd break up in between.

But there was something about the shy way in which he tucked his head as he danced, the quiet way he surrendered to the applause, and the look he gave me across the room, the look that said he truly saw me.

Something about that made me climb the stairs to my room and sit in the dark with my homework piled around me and weep.

For the way I missed home. For the way I had always missed home, even when I lived there.

And would Dad notice I was gone?

3

Keith

Africa: Brazzaville, Congo

1981–1983

> If only she could be so oblivious again, to feel such love without knowing it, mistaking it for laughter.
>
> Markus Zusak

Dad was gone on an orientation trip the day my mum gave birth to Keith, my jaundiced, five-pound brother on the outskirts of Brazzaville, Congo, in a small cement block house six weeks before he was due.

Dad had planned to go across the country to Pointe Noire to see various forms of agriculture, but when he reached Nkayi, about two hundred miles west of Brazzaville, Colonel Huguenin, the national leader of the Salvation Army, called him and told him he had a son, and Dad returned as fast as he could by train.

The day she gave birth, Mum would be bent over, like she was carrying a sack of charcoal, only it was me on her back in the

Gerry—a sturdy aluminum frame stretched with blue cloth that held my chubby form—during the long walk home from knitting bright yarn afghans with the local ladies, ladies who were blind, because my dad had signed us up with Christian Blind Mission. Mum hadn't signed up for anything, she told God in her prayers every morning over her cups of mint tea and Scripture faded yellow beneath her fingers.

I heard her. She didn't think I did, but I loved her more than life itself and I heard her from where I sat in my playpen Dad had made for me—about three feet square out of native African wood with green screen mesh for the sides—playing with Yogi Bear. But I wasn't able to say "I love you, Mummy, I'm sorry Mummy, I wish I could make you happy Mummy." I wasn't able to say anything, because I was eighteen months old and I'd stopped talking completely at thirteen months when we'd arrived in Congo, a French-speaking country. Words were confusing. They would tiptoe to the edge of my head but couldn't find the door.

So here I was and all I could do was almost walk and hug Mum's skinny knees and stare up at her big stomach and wait for the baby to arrive and for her to smile again.

I didn't remember Canada, except for some idea of snow, some kind of white cold film that Mum showed me in pictures. I wondered if it tasted like ice cream, which we only got when we traveled to the city.

I would crawl and grab fallen papayas from the ground in our backyard. They were yellow on the outside and reddish on the inside. Mum had taught me my colors, and everything here in Africa was bright: the trees with their wide banana leaves, the big red flowers, the sky, everything except for the dirt between my toes. And I would sit for hours by the fence in our backyard eating papaya, slippery juice between my fingers, after Mum had cut it up for me, watching my neighbors in their cotton dresses and long skirts and their French voices chattering and me wondering what it felt like to talk with someone. Mum always told me in a hushed voice not to stare, but they were so beautiful.

I had a friend. Her name was Zoe and she was my neighbor. She was really small because Mum said she didn't have much food, and she had beautiful black skin, a rich color that jumped like an exclamation point against her white teeth, and I saw her teeth a lot because she would laugh with all of them. And I wished I could make Mum laugh like that. I wished I could even make Mum smile, but she mostly just worked a lot.

I hoped maybe we would go back to the land of snow soon because I thought maybe we forgot Mum's smile there, when we were packing.

Mum liked to read. She had stacks of books and when I was having quiet time in my crib, she would sit in her wooden rocking chair and rock and read and sometimes then I would see her smile, just a little.

I liked to look at the pictures in my books but I didn't know my alphabet so the pictures spoke for me. So I'd trace the pictures like I was drawing them, like I could make the characters come to life and play with me but they just stayed there, stuck on that page and I would get sad and go find Zoe or Yogi.

I couldn't wait for the baby to be born because then Mum wouldn't be so tired all of the time, and maybe her face wouldn't be so very white. White wasn't a very nice color, I thought. Sometimes I would pinch my skin and try to turn it black like Zoe's because then my laugh would pop like hers did. Just kind of explode off my face. I didn't really know what I looked like because we didn't have any mirrors low enough for me to look in, but I would stand on the bathroom toilet when Mum wasn't looking and stretch up on my toes and look into the smudged reflection. But I didn't recognize myself. I looked so little. Mum's bowl-cut on my head and my round face and I wanted to look happy. So I pretended Zoe was my mirror when I was with her and I decided I wanted to be African.

That's why I stood for hours at the fence in our yard studying the people next door, pretending they were my family, until Dad came home from where he worked down the road, at the Blind Institute, and then we'd all have an afternoon siesta, Mum, Dad, and I.

And maybe the baby would be born black, because he was born in Africa. I hoped I wouldn't be jealous of him if he was, that I could love him the same even if he was the color I wanted to be, and then I decided I would be very proud of him indeed, my little African sibling, and I would take him around to all of my friends (which was one) and show him off.

And then Mum said he was coming.

But he was hurting her.

Her face was a bright sort of red when she told me, and she was trying not to cry, and her body was wrapped around her tummy and she was asking a local girl, who had just dropped off our mail, to take me to Zoe's even as our neighbor lady was running in and making Mum lie down. I wanted to stay. My eyes got wet and hot but I held my breath because Mum needed me to be strong, and I grabbed Yogi Bear and I asked God to send Daddy as soon as possible to help Mummy, Amen.

And I was carried into the hot African sun while Mum whimpered behind me like she was the baby and I felt very confused. I loved my sibling but was angry at him for making my mum hurt. And where was Daddy? And if Daddy wasn't here when we needed him to be, how did I know God would be? So I said another quick prayer in my head, telling God I would be the best little girl I could be if only he would bring home my dad that day to help Mum.

But he didn't.

Daddy didn't come home that day. He wouldn't arrive until the next day, but because the neighbor girl had miraculously showed up with the mail, she'd gone and found Mum a Finnish midwife who came and helped her with the birth, as well as a French doctor and a couple of nurses too.

But I wanted to help Mummy. And a little bit of me got angry, even as I was pretending to play with Zoe in the dirt outside her house. But all I could hear were Mum's screams, and then Zoe's mother called us inside and fed us some dry bread and sweet milk. But the windows, just horizontal panes of glass, were levered open and I could hear Mum, and I couldn't swallow that bread.

All I could do was hold Yogi and pat his back. Tell him in my head that everything was going to be all right, and I didn't notice my tears making him wet because I was too busy staring at the window thinking maybe if I stared hard enough Mum would feel me watching, would know that I wanted to be there for her.

Sometime later that day, when the sky was turning purple and the trees were wilting and everything smelled of jasmine, Mum stopped screaming and then I heard a smaller cry. I had been lying down on a braided mat in Zoe's house, having quiet time, and she was sleeping on another mat close to me, but I sat up straight when I heard that cry. I knew it was my sister or brother.

And it was so hard to wait, and finally Mummy sent the neighbor lady to come get me.

I didn't see anything except the mosquito netting where Mum lay. I didn't see the bloody rags or the midwife washing at the sink. I just saw Mum lying on that bed with a bundle on top where her stomach used to sit and the bundle was crying, more like mewing, and for a moment I wondered if she had accidentally given birth to a cat, and then I saw him. And he wasn't a cat, he was wrinkly and tiny and his eyes weren't open and his head was kind of smushed and his skin wasn't black, it was yellow. And he was beautiful.

Mum looked at me then and she smiled through the netting.

"Come here, Emily," she said, and I came. She drew me in with her free arm and she said, "This is your new baby brother. His name is Keith."

Keith smelled the way our laundry did when it came in from hanging in the sun, all warm and clean, and the midwife got me a stool and I sat beside Mum and petted Keith's skin. And something gurgled up inside of me and then sort of spilled over and I'm pretty sure my teeth laughed, my whole face wide and slung back because I had a friend in this bundle of cloth and Mum wasn't hurting anymore.

If only Daddy were here.

Daddy, who smelled like earth and sweat and spice. Daddy, with his lullaby, "The Lord Is My Shepherd," sung through the mosquito netting that tucked around my crib. Daddy, with his green eyes that shone behind his glasses and his beard that tickled my face when he kissed me on the cheek. Daddy, with his many friends who would take him away to do good things, but always at night he would read me a story before bed and pray with me and say he loved me.

And I had never seen Mum sadder than in Africa, even as Daddy had never been happier.

We were sitting in pails of water, Keith and I. Keith was one, and me, two and a half, and I still wasn't talking. We were naked and sitting there and we laughed a lot those days. The sun was making us brown like peanuts on plants, which grew all green and bushy, and Mum was in her garden bent over weeding things like collards, which Daddy also grew at the Blind Institute and which I thought tasted yucky.

We often sat in pails, Keith and I, because it was so hot, and then we'd run around chasing lizards. It was fun having a brother who could play with me.

Sometimes Daddy would strap Keith onto his back and take my hand in his and we'd walk the path to visit the neighbors. And sometimes he would keep Keith strapped on while he helped Mum weed the garden and I would run between the rows and feel the dirt between my toes and those were happy days.

I didn't watch the neighbors so much anymore because Keith was here, and Mum had her garden, and she wasn't so tired anymore. She made a lot of jam from papayas and mangoes, and the clean jars would wait all sparkling in the sun for her to slide the bright fruit into. And Dad would pick up French bread from the local bakery every day and he'd slice it on an angle and spread Mum's jam thick for us to eat.

Keith tipped over his pail, now, and he crawled across the dry cracked ground chasing what I thought was a lizard and I decided to stay a while longer in mine because it was so hot.

I was thinking again about those photographs of snow and I couldn't even remember what cold felt like when I heard it. Keith's scream.

It sounded like a gray parrot, his scream, followed by gasps and whimpers and I couldn't see him because he'd rounded the house into the clump of bushes, but I followed his cries.

Mum too, in her dirty apron and her brown hair all mussed and her blue eyes wide, and we found Keith lying in the bushes and a snake slithering away and Mum didn't say anything, which scared me more. She just picked Keith up and ran into the house. I followed because I could walk, even run now, and she was pulling things out of a cupboard and spreading cream on him and wrapping him in a bandage, his leg all bound in white gauze and he had a hard candy in his mouth and his eyes were bright and blue and that's when I cried.

I ran to him and hugged him. We ate French bread and cheese for supper and then we sat outside and waited for the big yellow sun to fall, like an egg, into the darkness.

Me with a hand in Keith's, and I would take care of him, I told myself. If only I had been there to pull him away from that snake he wouldn't be hurt, and I couldn't see it then but my face was lengthening, in the light of the setting sun.

Years later, when I was starving myself, Keith would draw a picture of me as a wrecking ball, destroying the wall of our family.

I had replaced my need to protect him with a need to protect myself.

And it was wrecking all of us.

4

The Beach

Canada: Blyth, Ontario

July 2007

> End? No, the journey doesn't end here. Death is just another path, one that we all must take. The grey rain-curtain of this world rolls back, and all turns to silver glass, and then you see it.
>
> J. R. R. Tolkien

And maybe I also wrecked Mum.

Maybe I'm somehow to blame for her brain cancer, for the grade-two malignant tumor, or "astrocytoma."

If I hadn't been so focused on myself she wouldn't have gotten hurt.

If I had been there when her own mother killed herself—Nanny, who had moved from England in 1996 to live beside us in a low-level house.

I'm holding Mum's hand in a room that smells of urine and sleep and unwashed skin, and the curtain is just a crimson blanket tacked to the window.

I walk to the window, lift the blanket, and let the light in. Beyond the glass are maple trees, and beyond those, the theater town of Blyth, all one thousand residents, and its bungalows. Mum and Dad live on the outskirts. The fields are dotted with low red barns and stretches of bean fields and corn and wheat. And cows, the dairy kind Dad grew up milking in the early morning, Scripture on his tongue for he never wanted to be a farmer. The Word was in his bones. His two older brothers, the strong silent type, just shook their heads at Ernest's hymns and his nose in the books.

I turn back to the room, to Mum's bed and the light shining on her face and she looks so peaceful, too peaceful, as though she'll just slide away from us, and there's spit in the corner of her mouth.

Beside her bed are bottles of face and foot cream, and I pick up the Oil of Olay, rub a coin-size dollop in my hand, softly trace her cheeks, and I sing to her, "Amazing Grace." And then I see them—her feet. They're moving. I stop singing, and her feet stop moving. I start again, and the blanket fidgets across her toes.

Mum's eyes are closed but she's stopped snoring, and her feet are keeping time with the song.

Dad's bowed in the garden, an overgrown tangle of root and weed that Mum used to keep immaculate. After massaging Mum's skin and changing her undergarments, an effort of hoisting and maneuvering because she is still asleep, I try to keep humming and notice the blanket's fallen back across the window. I run out the door. Standing in the light of July, the sadness from Mum's room just kind of falls off me, and Dad looks up.

"How's Mum?" he says, his knees digging into dirt and a pile of weeds beside him. He pushes up his glasses and I walk to him, pick up a trowel.

"Still sleeping."

He nods and yanks out a weed and I wish his forehead wasn't so wrinkled and I wish I could convince him that she is going to be okay, but it's been a month since I've returned home and she's slept more than she's been awake.

We're kneeling in the sun, praying with our posture, the lattice framing the yard and frogs singing in the pond. Mum is missing all of this, and it feels good to pull out the roots, dirt beneath my fingernails.

Dad clears his throat. "I just wanted to say thank you," he says.

I look at him. "For what?"

Dad doesn't do this. He doesn't talk about his feelings, and I've always wanted him to. Growing up, I would try to make him mad because then at least I'd see some emotion, but the most he ever did was pin me against the wall one day after I'd yelled in his face.

We are learning friendship, he and I. I'm learning that he is so much more than just my dad. He is a person, a man who feels misunderstood by most, who as a boy felt the unique call of ministry. He is a pastor who wants to please God, a father who gets confused about where ministry ends and family begins, and a husband who loves his wife more than life itself.

And so I'm doing this moment, slowly. My hands are pulling out weeds but my insides racing, all of the loveless places inside me clamoring for him to hug me and tell me he loves me because I'm needy this way. An affirmation junkie, some have said.

"Thank you for coming home," he says.

I think about the way he'd told me not to. The way he said he'd be fine even though I knew he wouldn't be. The way he'd asked me once to watch Mum from thousands of miles away, across the ocean in Korea, over webcam. He'd asked me because he had no one else, because no one else knew how bad it was or how to help a pastor who said he was fine. His wife asleep in a wheelchair in the aisle of the church.

Dad had been vacuuming and cleaning and doing the laundry. He'd been changing Mum and clipping her toenails and writing sermons and visiting people in the hospital and leading youth group and then rushing home to cook supper. He was not fine.

So I'd watched Mum over webcam, that one time, from Korea. And this is what I'd seen. I'd seen a woman who was dying. A woman wrapped in an afghan hunched over in her blue recliner, and if she'd slipped out of her chair or had tried to walk down the stairs or had needed someone to change her diaper I couldn't have done a single thing about it. All I could have done was call Dad's cell and he would have left youth group and driven home, and by that time it might have been too late.

This woman who had birthed all eight pounds of me, who'd labored me into the world, who'd nursed me and sung prayers over me and then, when I was eleven years old and rib and bone, had slipped into my bed when she thought I was sleeping just so she could hold me. Because during the day I wouldn't let her.

This woman who had baked us homemade bread and granola and taught us math and literature and geography at the kitchen table because she'd seen how I'd cried in the bathroom stall in kindergarten because I didn't understand the teacher, and had taken me home that day, had taken on the responsibility of teaching me.

This woman who sat slumped in a recliner hundreds of thousands of miles from me, dying. And I'd known I needed to go home.

I'd known, and yet my husband lay sleeping in the bedroom and I had three months of contract left. I had to go home yet I didn't want to, and Dad arrived then. I could hear the front door opening and then his footsteps and him turning the laptop, so I could see his face, grey like I'd never seen it, and he said, "I'm here now, Emily, thank you so much."

I had wanted to tell him then that I would be on the next plane. I had wanted to reassure him that I'd save him somehow but I knew my husband came first and so, "Goodnight, Dad," I said.

"Goodnight, Emily."

And now, Dad and I are yanking weeds and it feels like we are curing Mum somehow, like we are pulling out the tumor, but suddenly it isn't enough anymore. I want her to come out and shoo us away and kneel in the dirt and spend hours ministering to her flowers like she used to.

Dad is wiping his brow with the back of his hand and we're talking about flowers, Dad telling me their names because he's learned them since Mum got sick. He didn't use to care. It's why Mum spent so much time in her flowerbeds, for the hours Dad spent in his study or in the homes of parishioners or on the long commute to church. And now here he is, in the garden, while Mum sleeps.

I need to get away. It has been three days and Mum isn't rising and I miss my husband with a terrible soreness.

It doesn't help when I make supper and use too much spice and Dad says it doesn't taste good, and that's when I grab my guitar and the keys to the rusted old Chrysler, the minivan Mum and Dad bought in 1996 after the 1987 model died—the one Dad patched up with cardboard and duct tape when its window shattered the winter I was ten—and I drive to the grocery store and buy a bottle of wine.

The grocery store is Scranton's, and Mr. Scranton and his son are always there saying hello and walking the aisles. It's across from the post office where I bike every day to pick up Dad's bills and to chat with the ladies behind the desk, Sandra with her white bob and gentle smile, and Nora, with her quick laugh. And there's the convenience store kitty-corner, and then a long strip of Blyth's businesses, the hardware store, and a few restaurants that close down during winter and reopen in the summer for theater season.

And there's the Threshers Reunion Steam Show every September and the line of white trailers with their grey gypsies, as they are called, or nomadic seniors, and the old steam tractors and the smell of sausages and corn and the sound of fiddle music. Dad often does a big church meeting for the farmers, and his church—the one that meets in the school gym, the one I now attend—puts on a pie sale.

And I drive out of Blyth, turn right at the truck stop, drive past the apple orchards, the tree Trent and I will one day bike to and lie down and kiss under, and I drive twenty minutes to Goderich, to the beach.

Goderich was once called the prettiest town in Canada by Queen Elizabeth II. It's the town Dad says he might retire in someday, but we don't talk about someday a lot.

Goderich has more than one intersection, and a traffic circle known as The Square that is more of an octagon, with stores that don't close during winter. It has an IGA and a Walmart and a pub called Wicked Willie's, which will become Trent's and my favorite restaurant.

And it has three public beaches.

I drive down the sloping hill, lined with huge grey rocks, toward the stretch of blue and turn left, past the fish and chips stand, and drive alongside the boardwalk that stretches for over a mile. It's evening, but the sand is still covered in towels and picnics and families, the seagulls dipping. I decide to park near the entrance, by the rocks, because I want to be alone.

And that's where I uncork the bottle of Baby Duck, a cheap white that doesn't compare to the dessert wine Trent made when we lived in Edmonton, and I clean out a broken plastic cup I find in the backseat. Drink the wine slowly and cry a sort of almost-silent sobbing that sounds like the seagulls.

I didn't used to drink. Not until my honeymoon. Not until Halifax, Nova Scotia, where I had my first Alexander Keith's, an India Pale Ale. We drank the Keith's in a pizza joint overlooking Main Street, overlooking the bands and hippies and the smell of fish in the air. We drank right before we had the biggest fight of our marriage. Right before I told Trent that I no longer wanted children.

Maybe it had been the beer talking.

It had always been a sin to drink until I did, and then I realized people were afraid of alcohol and I didn't want to be afraid. I knew God was bigger than a beer and that it wasn't about the beer, it was about too many beers.

I try not to fill the plastic glass too many times and I write a song for Mum, on a pad of yellow paper I pull from my handbag. I pick up my un-tuned guitar, put the words to melody, and sing to the sound of the waves and the gulls, dipping.

You're sitting there looking at me
With your big blue eyes and your coffee and
I wonder
Do you see me?

Dancing around, laughing out loud
With your hands held high and your head slightly
Bowed
And I wonder
Where's the music?

When the sky turns blue and the
Waves roll in
When I open my eyes in the morning
Will you be here?

You're sitting there
Looking at me
With your big blue eyes and your coffee
And I wonder
Do you see me?

Dancing around
Laughing out loud with your hands held high
And your head slightly bowed
And I wonder
Where's the music?

When the sky turns blue and the waves roll in
When I open my eyes in the morning
Will you be here?

Tomorrow holds its breath
I hug you tight
Close the door

Whisper goodnight and I wonder
Will you be here?

The next morning I am lying in bed, the one with the broken spring, the frogs singing through my window. A green choir, those thick-throated bulls, and sunlight is pooling on the floor through the bent blinds when I hear slippers padding down the stairs. Slow, methodical, and a knock at my door.

"Come in." I sit up, and the door swings open.

It is Mum.

She is awake.

She is here.

She's wearing her purple robe, and she holds a teacup in her hand and it wobbles and hot tea dribbles down her hand and she has a smile on her face.

"Good morning, Beautiful," she says, her slippers padding across the floor.

I just stare at her. At the way her eyes are so blue in her face, so open. At the blush in her cheeks. She is thin and pale and her robe hangs loose but she is standing, walking, and setting the cup of Earl Grey in my palms and then reaching into her pocket. "Ta da!" she says with a laugh, pulling out a banana.

It's my breakfast.

I laugh too, put the banana and tea on the side table with its photo of Trent and my leatherbound Bible, and I pull her close. She smells like lotion, and I could cry. For the way everything seems so normal.

"Thank you, Mum," I say into her hair.

She nods, pats my cheek, and sits down on the bed.

"I'm so glad you're here, Emily," she says. "I've missed you, Sweet Pea."

She knows who I am. She remembers my childhood nickname and I don't know how long I have. How long until her mind goes fuzzy and she starts to hum and click her tongue and mumble. But for now, I ask her.

"Is it hard, Mum? Is it hard to be asleep so long, and to miss so many days?"

She looks at me. Her eyes clear and round.

"Yes," she says. "It's hard because then I don't get to see you. But I'm so glad you're here. Do you know that?"

"I know that, Mum."

She nods happily.

"I pray for you when I'm sleeping," she says then.

"You do?"

"I pray that you'll know how much I love you," she says. She's starting to hum and she's looking tired.

I kiss her on her cheek. "I love you too, Mum."

She shakes her head. "I love you, bigger."

Then she laughs and sighs and stands up, falls back down, and I gently prop her up.

She turns. "Don't forget, it's Coffee Break today."

I shake my head. "Mum, you slept through Coffee Break. That was yesterday. It's Thursday."

Her blue eyes are worried. "No, no, it's Wednesday today, I have my bag all ready and I just have to find my Bible and my glasses. The calendar says it's Wednesday."

"Thank you for breakfast, Mum," I say, because I'm not sure if she'll be awake when I come upstairs.

"Anytime, sweetie," she says, padding her way out the door, the frogs singing and the sunshine pooling on the floor.

Maybe later. Maybe later I'll ask her if she's angry at God, after the banana and the sweet tea, because Mum always puts in an extra scoop of sugar, and me changing and climbing the stairs. She's singing a hymn while she's trying to pull on her pants in the bedroom and she won't let me help her this morning. She wants to do it all by herself but it will take her hours, and her blue bag is packed by the door with her Bible and her glasses.

Dad's already in the study, because it's sermon writing day, and the computer is reminding Mum that it's Mocha Time. It's 10 a.m. and that's when Mum has her mocha and Dad has rigged the computer to tell her so he doesn't have to, and I'm proud of him for this. But it makes me jump a little too: his voice, blurting out through the speakers, and then it's Lunch Time and Nap Time, and at three o'clock, Tea Time.

I check my email and Trent's in Thailand. He's at a festival on the beach and Mum is singing off-key in her bedroom and there's a pile of urine-soaked sheets to wash and I cry, sitting there, at the computer.

Mum finds me shoving sheets into the washing machine.

"You must miss him," she says, putting a hand on my shoulder. Her pants are backwards, but they're on. She's done it all by herself. "Did I tell you about the first time your dad and I kissed?"

She has, but I ask her to tell me again because she also thinks it's Wednesday, and because she missed Coffee Break, slept right through it, and I can't bear to disappoint her twice.

"There was a shooting star," she says. "We were at the farm and we kissed beneath the shooting star."

And I think about how Mum used to shrug out of Dad's embrace when we were kids, how she'd turn away and he would look down.

When did they stop kissing beneath shooting stars?

That night, after I make macaroni and cheese and broil the cheese and tomatoes on top, like Mum used to do, we sit and we eat—all three of us, Mum only taking a few mouthfuls and then playing with her pills and humming.

Then she and Dad tuck beside each other on the couch under an afghan, touching toes and watching British comedy. I pause for a minute by the door; see the way Mum is nestled against Dad's arm and the way he feeds her yogurt.

And they're laughing together.

Mitchell, Ont.
Oct. 17, 1984

The children and I went for a walk this morning to get the mail, and I realized how good they are, how much companionship they give me and each other and how much we need to do little things like walks together.

Reading Maxine Hancock's book, **Love Knows No Difference**; time given to others in the Lord's work is given back to us! This is a new concept for me. I know if I give things, that God provides us with what we need, but I didn't think we could ever get back time spent. I would like to give it a try, for I feel the Lord wants me to spend more time alone with Him. I always claim I have too many other things to do, but if I bring the needs before Him, I know He will help me.

Finding Jesus

Canada: Edmonton and Neerlandia, Alberta

Fall 1998

> I once listened to an Indian on television say that God was in the wind and the water, and I wondered at how beautiful that was because it meant you could swim in Him or have Him brush your face in a breeze.
>
> Donald Miller

When I was eight I would scrunch my eyes shut and try to picture God. It was so hard to pray because I didn't know who I was praying to.

I've been an artist all my life. A visual learner. A girl who needs a picture to believe and there is no photograph of Jesus, no snapshot of God the Father.

There is the crucifix at the front of the church, but the Jesus that hangs there is dead.

And it wasn't Jesus I needed at eight years old. It was a father. So it was Jesus's father I prayed to.

I would sit in bed and close my eyes so tight they'd hurt and then I'd feel guilty for trying to see God because shouldn't my faith be stronger than that?

But I couldn't stop trying and one day, God became an old grandfather type in my mind and I prayed to that face. That kindly, bearded, safe face.

Soon, though, I stopped eating.

I didn't know about anorexia. I just knew that an elderly friend of mine had died, a friend I called Grandma Elsie, a woman who had loved me, who had wanted to spend time with me, who had played cards and sipped tea with me. My other grandparents lived far away. Elsie had died, and I didn't know how to handle death. Or loneliness.

I had no choice at home about anything. I was expected to take care of my siblings. Mum read my journal and Dad didn't ask me how I was doing and we moved ten times before I turned seven.

So I stopped eating.

I stopped eating when I turned nine and got sick with the flu. Mum and I had gone to visit Nanny in London, England. While I was there, my face flushed and my weight dropped because of the virus, and I thought I'd never looked prettier.

And for all of my wanting attention because Dad was so busy trying to provide for us after Africa, working at the skim milk factory while going to seminary and becoming a pastor, and Mum was so tired from having babies—giving birth to two more girls when we returned home from Congo and homeschooling us on a shoestring budget—my lengthening face stopped smiling.

And the picture of God in my head became a man who was always serious and studying unless he was at church where he smiled and laughed with people for hours. He still read us stories, but I don't remember ever playing with my dad.

And when I got tired of pretending everything was okay, I got the flu in England and came home with an eating disorder.

Mum took me to get blood tests because I wasn't eating and I was always angry and going to bed at eight or earlier and the doctors said what I needed was school.

But what I needed was love, to wrap me up in its arms and tell me how beautiful I was and to make me laugh.

I needed a love that smiled.

And I needed to know that God wasn't my dad or my mum, but when you're little, he is. He is the face of your loved ones. But your loved ones make mistakes. And God doesn't.

That isn't something you can see, though, when you're nine years old. Yet there are always glimpses.

There are those nights when your dad reads an extra story or sings one more song. There are those thunderstorms when your mum lights candles and you all stand on the back porch and count the Mississippis after the rumble until the sky cracks with light. There are fresh homemade carrot cakes baked for your birthday and homemade stockings stitched with your name on them and home-sewn dresses out of red velvet and there's your dad making you and your sisters a playhouse in the woods.

There are family trips in the tent trailer to the Maritimes and there are pets: Misty, my cat, and then our dogs: Argus, a yellow lab, and Christy, a quiet black Newfoundland who laid down when she ate.

There is cross-country skiing and tapping maple trees and going square dancing. There is hot maple syrup on snow and there's the Harvest Festival.

But when you're young, you see the gaps more than you do the glimpses. You see the hole more than the donut.

And my prayers became these long forced things I spouted late at night to the wall beside my bed while my stomach rumbled because I knew enough to believe in God. I knew we needed something holy and big and awesome like a creator to make this world, to make us, as people, but I didn't know him.

And I blamed God because it was in his name that I had to

wear leotards to church. It was in his name that my father was so distracted. It was in his name that we had to move so often.

And then at thirteen, when I was dying on the hospital bed and the nurses said I was a miracle, I finally saw him.

I saw God for who he was—a Savior who wasn't a minister with a wrinkled forehead stuck in his office, who wasn't a mother who had never been affirmed growing up, who wasn't the church with all of its rules.

He was grace. And I began to believe with more than my mind, because I wanted to live.

I wanted to date boys. I wanted to go on mission trips and see the world, but I didn't want to talk about those four years. I didn't want to talk about my wounds, the ones that had caused the anorexia.

And my parents didn't talk about it either because we all just wanted to move on.

I still didn't understand God the Father. And Jesus became the grace I spoke to but never let get too close.

And then, the Bible school in Edmonton.

There were forty students in the class, and there was New Testament and Old Testament and the Psalms and Apologetics, and there was doing English as a Second Language (ESL) and tutoring and sports ministry.

And Jesus took on the face of my professors, in particular, Zane, who read my poetry and told me I had a gift but that I had to slow down. I had to take time to edit and prune, but I laughed at him. I didn't have time for editing.

And my friend Donna and I left encouraging notes in everyone's mailboxes. We made videos after school, and we watched *Anne of Green Gables* on the weekends and did belly laughs. And Jesus became the belly laugh.

He became my roommates Alex and Meg, who worried about me because I'd eat crackers and cheese most nights for supper, and hide in my room doing homework all hours. And they asked me one night to go study with them and some other students at the local pub and I actually brought my textbooks. And when I saw Alex's glass of amber liquid I asked her if it was apple juice. And she looked at me with laughing eyes and said, "Yes, Emily, I'm drinking apple juice in a bar."

And Jesus became the face of Trent. He became the handsome rugged face of a farm boy from Neerlandia, Alberta, who had long legs and kind eyes. He became the shy figure who showed up on my doorstep in his army uniform because he was in the reserves, the boy who asked me to go for a walk in the hills behind the townhouses.

"Do you want to ask me out?" I said to him on our walk, on our way home.

He laughed. Looked down. "Do you want to go out with me, Emily?"

I wanted to kiss him right there, kiss the dimples in his cheeks, but I also wanted this one to be different. Trent was different from all of the other boys I'd dated. He was pure and clean and good. He wasn't anti-Christian like the boy I'd loved in high school. He wasn't Seth who had wanted me to take off my pants. He wasn't twenty-one-year-old Eric who'd been dating someone else when he'd given me my sweet sixteen kiss.

No, Trent was a Christian Reformed boy from a Dutch town who played sports and volunteered at Kids Club and drove an old, long blue car called The Beast. He was a camp kid who hung out with his sisters and went bowling with his grandma.

"Yes," I said. "I want to go out with you."

He had to leave then, in The Beast, but we held hands every day after that.

And sometimes we'd lie on my bed in my narrow closet of a room, with those classroom scraps of poetry clinging to my walls and art from high school and postcards from friends and home. We'd listen to Bon Jovi or Matchbox Twenty and we'd talk.

About things like Christmas trees. How they had to be real. It wasn't a Christmas tree if it wasn't real and he taught me the difference between a spruce and a pine.

And then Trent took me home.

He introduced me to his mom, Marge, who hugged me and made us Oh Henry squares and to his dad, Harvey, who looked like a shorter version of Trent, who was quiet and wise and gruff and to his sisters, Teneale and Teshah, who were fun and athletic and laughed a lot.

The first time I met his Grandma Wierenga, she kissed me straight on the lips the way the Dutch do.

Trent and I wouldn't kiss for six months. And when we did, he'd find the lip of my ear, lying there on that single bed, and then we'd stand, because we wanted our first kiss to be vertical.

And when he left that night he tripped over a crack in the sidewalk because he'd been floating, he'd tell me later, and he went home and made me a card. Using construction paper. Writing, "Thank you for the kiss" in magic marker.

I've kissed a lot of boys. And you can tell about a kiss like you can tell about a good beer. I've had Pilsners. I've had Molson's. But Trent's kiss was a Rickard's Red—my favorite.

More than ten years later he still pulls me close in patches of sunshine as we walk. But a couple of times, I've pulled back. Stiffened.

And it isn't because of him, the father of my children, the man who's held me for a decade beneath a duvet, the man who dances in our living room and wrestles with our boys and makes me milkshakes with vanilla and strawberries.

It is because of me, because of the way Mum used to pull back from Dad when he tried to kiss her.

As though she couldn't believe he would want to.

Perhaps it's because Trent is able to enjoy a kiss, to separate himself from the rest of the day and enter fully into my lips. But I bring all of me with it. All of my insecurities about my hips, my lips, my heart, my mind, and my neglected childhood. Sometimes I fake it. Sometimes I'm able to just enjoy it, but sometimes, the sunlight makes shadows on the ground and I notice my silhouette and the way my shoulders hunch and I wonder if I'll ever look confident and this makes me slouch further. And I wonder what he sees in me.

But Trent waits for those pools of light. He wants to see all of me. And even as I pull away, he tries again, and I see him, for who he is: love. The First Corinthians kind.

"I'm proud of you," he tells me, then.

The trees touching the sky.

And my shoulders straighten even as his mouth touches mine.

6

Losing Faith

Canada: Vancouver, British Columbia

May 1999

> We are not human beings having a spiritual experience. We are spiritual beings having a human experience.
>
> Pierre Teilhard de Chardin

It was spring, and we sang songs in the blue and purple school bus, Donna and I, as we drove Highway 16 out of the city and through Jasper, with its wildlife signs and the Old Indian face carved into the rock.

I didn't know then how many trips Trent and I would end up taking to Jasper.

How the mountains would become my tabernacle.

How every time we approached the Canadian Rockies Trent would turn to me and say, "Can you imagine being pioneers, years ago? Can you imagine how much time and energy it took to carve roads out of these rocks?"

And me rolling my eyes and laughing. Us parking by the lake, shallow up to our ankles for meters, the water a turquoise blue, and taking our boys on our shoulders for a splash. Camping at Snaring River, snowboarding Marmot, hiking Maligne Canyon, and weeping over the Ghost Glacier of Mt. Edith Cavell.

But for now Trent sat in the back of the bus with his best friend Lane, and they were probably lighting their farts on fire, while Donna and I talked about wanting to marry missionaries who saved the world.

I liked Trent.

I liked him so much I'd planned a scavenger hunt for him on Valentine's. His friends had dressed up in trench coats and top hats, and had stationed themselves all over the city. They'd smoked cigars and told Trent the next clue, until finally he'd arrived at The Snuggery Café where I'd had a huge card waiting for him, and a table for two by the window. And we'd shared giant cookies and hot chocolate.

But I didn't think I would marry him.

I was eighteen and I wanted to marry someone who wore funky ties and played the guitar and wrote poetry on the steamed-up bathroom mirror for me and saved orphans in Africa.

Trent wanted to become a teacher and he wore T-shirts and jeans and he was a jock who didn't wax poetic.

"Maybe you and I can start a school together," I said to Donna, an East Indian girl from Saskatoon, a slim sweet girl with an easy laugh. "We can teach writing and feed hungry children and tell them about Jesus."

Jesus was a magical word in Bible school. If you said his name with a certain amount of reverence you were really profound. Donna and I were both really profound.

"Yes!" she said. "We can live next door to each other and drink tea in the evenings on our porches and our children can play together. And we'll help people."

We didn't know then that she'd be the one to move overseas with her husband while I stayed in Canada and fostered children. We didn't know that Jesus's name wasn't magical, that it was hard, and that it meant trouble in this world, but to take heart because he had overcome.

All we knew was that the bus was driving Highway 16 through Jasper to Vancouver and we were going to be doing inner city ministry.

It was a one-year program, Mount Carmel, and we'd had our graduation, Donna and I singing up front and both of us earning top marks while Trent's townhouse of six boys failed, all but him, and this was the annual mission trip.

It had been a year of choir concerts and potlucks and early morning devotions. It had been a year of breaking, of watching a video on Mother Teresa and her work in India, and me running outside to the hill beyond the school and falling on the grass and weeping for all of the pain and all of the need.

It had been a year of excavating Scripture and kissing a farm boy in the rain, and ice skating. It had been a year of memorizing verses and the lines in each other's palms.

Trent and I eventually sat together on the bus, crossing the Alberta border into BC and onto Highway 5 and stopping in Kamloops for Dairy Queen Blizzards. We held hands, his calloused and strong, and he told me about traveling to Yellowstone National Park with his family in the summer and how the three kids would ride in the back of the truck on a mattress and play cards.

He told me about his Grandpa Neumann who ran the Vega Ferry for years, about his Papa Wierenga who died when Trent was six but Trent could still remember him doing magic tricks.

"My granddad was a police officer," I said, "and Nanny was a watercolor artist." Yet Trent had grown up in the same farmyard as his grandparents, while mine had lived across the ocean.

And I wondered if he was dangerous enough. Because I wanted more than a country corner and a family. I wanted to get as far away from family as possible, not because I didn't love them, but because I didn't know, yet, how much I needed them. I was confused, about

God and myself, and I needed to know who I was and who God was. Without all of my dad's sermons and my mother's Christian books and Serenity Prayer wall hangings.

So Trent and I laced hands in the backseat of the bus while I pictured a future without him.

We had arrived in BC the night before, and were visiting the Ling Yen Mountain Temple, a Hindu temple in Richmond, to pray over the grounds, over the false religion, over the spirits and the misguided worshipers, but I found myself taking off my shoes, instead.

We had spent the night at Westminster Gospel Chapel in Burnaby, in the basement, the girls piled into one Sunday school room in our sleeping bags, and the boys in another.

We would stay there all week, cooking our meals in the church kitchen and making sandwiches each morning to take on the streets. And today was temple day, learning the different religions and beliefs of Vancouver, and there were shoes lining the rug outside the holiest of places I had seen. Candles alight within and men and women prostrate before golden gods.

And I stood there with my long blonde hair and my bell bottoms, the jeans I always wore, wondering why we didn't remove our shoes at church. Why I had never felt this kind of holiness at church, why we didn't prostrate ourselves before the Living God, and who was to say they weren't right and we weren't wrong?

They seemed even more convicted than any of the church members I had encountered in any of the United Churches my father had preached at, and so I took off my shoes and I stopped believing.

I had flirted with disbelief for years, in those fleeting moments: the ones where your butt goes numb on the pew or you watch too many sad stories on the news or you overhear a parishioner gossiping about your family. Just a moment's worth of disbelief, but eventually it adds up to an hour, and on this particular day it all just sort of piled up and knocked me over. And it was enough to make me take off my shoes.

We hadn't even begun evangelizing yet, and there I was, not even praying anymore.

And I don't know but that I didn't feel lighter somehow. I no longer had an agenda when I was sitting with the homeless in the park on East Hastings Street, cigarette butts and needles on the grass, and men and women in their trench coats and dirty T-shirts on the benches, and me sharing my sandwiches with them.

And I wasn't preaching Jesus to them because I wasn't even praying that week. No, I was just eating with a man named Aaron who was in his twenties and had been evicted from his apartment because he couldn't pay rent, who smoked weed in the park and ate soup across the street at Pastor Gloria's Living Waters Mission.

And I didn't have any magical words to say, like "Jesus loves you." Instead, I had a sandwich to give him and I didn't feel worried when I left over whether or not I had said the right thing.

Instead, I felt full because a day spent feeding the hungry is true religion. We'd been given tracts to hand out but I'd stuffed them in my pockets. I was tired of pretending things were okay when they weren't. I was tired of pat answers and cozy Scripture verses. I wanted to know what was real, even if it meant being a heathen.

By the end of the week we'd sorted clothes at a distribution center, served hot dogs on fancy china to the homeless, and participated in a charismatic church service where people fell on the floor. We served soup and cleaned out a ministry space, and then, the last night, I called home.

I talked to Mum for a few minutes and she said, "Emily, can I ask you what's been going on this week?"

"Well, I thought I just told you," I said, not understanding.

"No, I mean, has something else been going on? Because God has woken me up every single night to pray for you," Mum said.

I nearly took off my shoes right then and there.

And suddenly the shaky scaffolding of my faith re-erected itself. My doubts disappeared in light of a God who was bigger than all of my questions. A God who cared. About me.

"Oh Mum," I said into the receiver. "I stopped believing this week," and it didn't matter that she was the wife of a minister. She was my mum and she had risen every night to pray for me.

"God loves you, sweetie," she said. "He'll always love you. And he woke me every night this week because he loves you. We might not get it right, honey, but he always will."

God will always get it right. He is the one who sets burning bushes alight. He is the one who gives us holy ground. No matter where we are, if God is there, the earth is sacred.

I didn't have it all figured out. I knew I would always hate tracts. I knew I would always fight the institution. I would always wonder at the holiness I'd felt in the temple that day, but maybe holiness is found in our hungering for God and those people were hungering. They were just missing the cross. And God loved them and he met them in their hunger.

And he'd met me in mine, in my anorexic starvation, and he was meeting me now, in the middle of the night through the prayers of my mother.

And I really didn't know what to do in the face of that kind of love.

Except lean in and kiss it quietly.

7

Apology

Central America: Ensanada, Mexico

May 1999

> The poverty in the West is a different kind of poverty—it is not only a poverty of loneliness but also of spirituality. There's a hunger for love, as there is a hunger for God.
>
> Mother Teresa

From Vancouver, some went home.

Trent and I were among the ten who remained and then flew from Vancouver to San Diego, California, where we slept overnight in a church basement and rented a van. And that's when Trent and I learned we weren't allowed to date in Mexico.

Victor, the school president with the clipped grey moustache, asked to talk with us at a rest stop at the border. He walked with a quick step to the side of the convenience store. It had been two days of travel, and the air clung like sticky secrets. My shirt was damp against my skin and all I wanted was to step into that store with its air conditioning.

"I'm going to have to ask you two to pretend you're not dating when we're on this trip," Victor said and I snapped to attention. "We're on a mission trip, and I don't want any fooling around, so are you willing to commit to not dating for a week?"

"What does that mean, exactly?" said Trent, who was diplomatic and calm. "Can we still sit beside each other in the van?"

Victor shook his head. "I'm sorry, no."

This made my head spin because we weren't even witnessing to anyone in the van. It was just us and the team and they knew we were together.

"There's no holding hands or kissing or sitting next to each other, or talking privately," he continued.

I didn't say anything. I just nodded and then turned and walked straight into the store and stuck my head in the fridge with all of the bottles of Gatorade and water staring at me. I tried to count to ten, and then twenty, but no amount of numbers were helping.

Eventually I pulled my head out and walked back to the van, my long hair sticking to the back of my neck and Trent seated in the far corner beside Jimmy, and then Meg beside Jimmy, and so I sat in the middle seat beside Patrick with the curly hair and Donna.

We passed Rosarito Beach, thirty-five minutes south of the border, and there were palm trees and coconuts; there were donkeys and slums and resorts, the air tasting like sweat and limes.

I should have been happy.

But all year long I'd been bothered by our president, who was so serious and formal and disciplined. He reminded me of my dad, an authoritarian figure who, when I asked him for something, would often say "No" without explaining or budging. And if my mother was upset at me, which she was a lot because I would often talk back, she would ask Dad to spank me and he would, with his hand or a wooden spoon or his belt.

When I was twelve the counselor asked Dad to describe who I was, my likes and dislikes, and he couldn't. That's what made him start trying.

And so after I was hospitalized for three months and put on twenty pounds and no longer looked like I'd been a resident in a concentration camp, Dad and I began to "date." Little dates, to Ann's Café where they served large cinnamon buns and mugs of hot cocoa. And it was hard at first, because Dad was scared of saying the wrong thing and making me relapse and I was wary of Dad, knowing he was doing this because the counselor had told him to, but it was something.

Sometimes all you need is something, but Victor reminded me of my father before Ann's Café, the man who'd never had time for me, who'd only had time for rules.

So the old Emily kept trying to rear her head, the angry little girl inside of me who'd never been heard. And I kept shoving her down, telling her to be quiet or she'd make a fool of herself. But she was getting restless.

We stayed in missionary headquarters outside of Ensenada, a coastal city just seventy-five miles from the US border, the girls in one room with bunk beds lining the walls and the boys in another and a large sitting room where the boys wrestled and the girls wrote in their journals or played cards.

The first few days we took the van over to the building that we were working on, a secondary headquarters for missionaries, and we spent all day in the sun mixing and plastering and drinking water.

At lunch the couple who ran the place, a Mexican man and his wife, made us hot rice with beans and tortillas, Trent and I making sure we didn't sit beside each other, but there were a couple of times when we talked, he and I, finding quiet places behind a building or a tree.

During one of those times we discussed past relationships. He'd kissed two girls, he said. And then he asked me what I'd done with other boys. How far I'd gone.

And I told him there, our necks browning in the sun, him sitting on a green plastic chair and me pacing the ground before him.

I told him about Seth and Eric and Brad and Greg and on—too many of them—and how they'd never made it all the way but I still felt like what the church would call damaged goods.

And Trent sat very quietly and it was one of the few times I'd see his eyes get wet. The tears didn't fall, but they sat in the corners of his eyes and he said he needed to think.

Me, twisting my purity ring as I walked away, leaving a white mark on my finger when I tried to pull it off because it felt like a lie.

Victor somehow got word of us talking, alone, and he asked us to meet him in the dining hall and that's when the little girl inside of me made herself known.

"I thought I'd asked you two not to spend time together this week," Victor said.

"We were just talking," said Trent.

"But you were alone, and it's not proper on mission trip."

"Who are you to tell us we can't talk?" I said then. My face reddened and all I saw was my dad. All I saw was a man who didn't know me. Who was giving me rules I couldn't keep and I wanted to please him but was so tired of trying. Who told me it was for my own good, but there was nothing good about it, there was no love in it.

"This is ridiculous!" I said then, yelling, and I knew Trent was stiffening even as I looked at Victor. "We are not soldiers to be commanded around. We are real people and we are adults and we are in a relationship. So please stop telling us how to live our lives!"

I don't think Victor's moustache moved once and Trent touched my shoulder with his hand and I shrugged it off and I ran. Because that's what I do. I run, because I can't face the way I've just hurt someone, and because I'm not ready to say sorry yet.

And so I ran past the building we were fixing up, my friends sitting and drinking iced tea because we were done for the day, and I ran past the building where Trent and I had talked, and I just kept running, past a field where kids were playing soccer and then I found a palm tree and I leaned there and I cried. Forgetting all about the warning of tarantulas and snakes. Forgetting everything except the shame of a little girl who'd shouted at her school president, and I knew I was wrong and that I'd have to walk back there and apologize.

So I sat by that tree, that tall palm with its gracious leaves, and stared up through the slits of green and slowly my sobs mended into prayers.

And Trent met me as I walked back down that gravel road, the sun sinking fast and the kids done with their soccer game. He just stopped me there on the gravel and pulled me close. And he held my shame like it was a bird with a broken wing and he gave that bird flight. The shame, a flash of red in the sky and then it was gone.

Everyone was piling into the van, heading back to the dorms, and I found Victor and asked to speak to him. I stuttered, "I'm sorry."

Victor shook his head and his eyes were watery behind his rims. "I'm sorry too," he said.

We hugged awkwardly then.

It was the sorry I'd never gotten from my dad.

But for now, this was enough.

This hug in Ensenada.

The following day we visited a church where there were no seats, only people standing and raising their hands and worshiping, a man on a guitar with a broken string and voices, a choir of earth's poorest raising the roof of heaven. I looked behind me as they sang, out the open door, and there was field upon field, small tin-roofed houses, and chickens and men hunched over their gardens and women with children.

They had nothing. And yet they sang with everything: with their hands and their arms and with all of their hearts.

And afterward I held a little girl who peed on me because she had no diaper and the kids, with their dirty faces, standing around, giggling, caressing our white skin and then running away.

I was frustrated, not being able to speak in Spanish, but just smiled a lot and held the children with their brown shoeless feet and told them they were beautiful.

Then we were piling back into our van, the children running alongside, waving. And I wondered what would happen to them. Would they end up on the streets selling colorful bead necklaces and ponchos? Would their backs be bent from harrowing rows in their garden? Would they preach in a one-room church with no pews or chairs? And why couldn't we help them?

But their faces were smiling and I knew it was us who needed help.

It was our last day there, and we would spend one more night in the bunk beds and then drive back to San Diego, past Rosarito Beach and we would stop there, would strip off our socks and our shoes and run into the water—Jimmy leading the way in just his boxers and then, being Jimmy, known for his mooning, he took off his shorts in the ocean and swung them over his head and then yelped as the water pulled his shorts away. And he was left with just the ocean lapping at his pale skin.

Trent gave him his shirt to wrap around, and I loved him right there and then. Because he was never too big to act with small gestures, gestures that said *I see you. I care about you. Let me be your friend.*

And it was these Good Samaritan gestures that healed people. And one day they would heal me too.

8

Nanny

Canada: Edmonton, Alberta; Echo Bay, Ontario

June 1999

> Do not abandon yourselves to despair. We are the Easter people and hallelujah is our song.
>
> John Paul II

I received the phone call in the kitchen of Trent's townhouse.

I had just finished my shift at McDonald's next to Capilano Mall and had walked three blocks to Trent's, past the massage parlor with its drawn drapes and the line of townhouses with children's toys littering the lawns.

Trent and I had been lying in his room, the one overlooking the parking lot, kissing on his bed when Sam, one of his five roommates, knocked on the door and said the phone was for me.

Dad's voice on the other end, as I stood in the corner of the kitchen between the fridge and the table, the counter stacked with empty pizza boxes and dirty dishes.

At first I didn't think I'd heard him right. Trent's roommates were in the living room on the PlayStation and all I could make out was Nanny, suicide, funeral, and my British grandmother was dead.

Dad saying Mum had found her, in the bathtub, and the funeral was on Saturday, and he would pay for me to come home.

"Of course," I said, and then I began to cry thinking about Mum finding Nanny.

"Oh, poor, poor Mum," I kept saying into the receiver. That's all I could think. Because Mum had taken care of Nanny for the past three years since she'd moved from England.

And there had been no note.

I hung up the phone in a fog, stumbled up the stairs to where Trent lay on his wrinkled duvet, and I just stood there until he put down his book and looked up. "What's wrong?" he said.

My clothes smelled like French fries.

"My Nanny," I said. "She's . . . dead. Mum found her. I have to go home."

Going home is hard, because it means revisiting the person you used to be, but when your mum is grieving the loss of a mother she found in a bathtub, it's even harder.

And you want to be the bigger person. You want to take your grieving mother's hand and tell her it's going to be fine, but it won't be. You can't resurrect the dead, because that would make you Jesus. All you can do is ask God to resurrect a person's hope, while eating chocolate in your old room, on the double bed, staring up at posters of Michael W. Smith and DC Talk.

You eat chocolate and then you pick out an outfit for the funeral and you try to think religious thoughts about the deceased. But all you can think is, *Why did she have to be so selfish?*

And you know suicide is more complex than that.

But you also know the reason Nanny made the decision to end her life with a razor is because two weeks earlier, Mum and Dad had told her that they were moving. Dad was being transferred. And Nanny didn't want to move because that would mean putting her in a retirement home, or assisted living.

Upstairs, now, Mum has set the urn with Nanny's ashes on the piano, where Allison sits playing hymns, and Mum is making supper. Tonight it will be chili with rice and zucchini chocolate cake for dessert, and Mum isn't crying and you wonder if she's allowed herself to. Or maybe she's too hurt or shocked or angry to cry. And how do you tell your mother that she has your permission to cry?

So you joke around with your brother and he's sarcastic back.

"Nice sweater," you tell him, even though you secretly like it.

"Nice face," he says back.

Meredith is on the carpet by the piano doing a puzzle and she giggles then looks guilty for feeling happy, and Allison keeps playing hymns, "How Great Thou Art" and "It Is Well" and then Mum leaves the kitchen and heads down the hall to her bedroom and closes the door. Outside, Dad is mowing the lawn.

And we all grow quiet but we hear nothing save for the mower, and now we're scared. Because death makes a person anxious like that.

After a while, Mum emerges from the bedroom and we breathe again. She looks weary and I can tell she's cried and we all awkwardly try to comfort her and she nods and smiles, and Dad comes in smelling like grass and we eat chili.

Just a few months before, at Christmas, Nanny had been there in our living room. She had brought a bulging bag full of gifts and she'd played Santa Claus, in her dark green cardigan and her long black skirt, and she'd handed out those gifts with glee.

Then she'd given us sweater-jackets that she had knit. Mine was green. And they'd smelled like cigarette smoke and musky perfume because that was Nanny.

And I'd always liked visiting her house, the one-story flat she'd bought to go on the land beside ours when she'd moved from

England. Her living room full of Asian artifacts and watercolor paintings on the walls, and she'd listened to classical music while knitting on the sofa. It was like a museum of her life, her house, and it was elegant and expensive and mysterious.

And then Dad—who'd been working part-time and commuting two hours—had accepted a full-time job in southern Ontario, and two weeks later Mum had found Nanny dead in the bathtub.

For years, all I've been able to feel is angry.

Maybe it's because when I'm not angry, I let myself remember Nanny and I miss her. The sorrow is like a cavern I keep falling into and the anger keeps me out of there, away from there, safe.

Maybe it's because Mum had faithfully visited and cared for Nanny, daily, because Mum hoped that through her actions Nanny would fall in love with Jesus too.

Or maybe it's because, three years after finding her mother in the bathtub, a cancerous tumor appeared on my mum's brain.

And after returning home from Korea, I read an article that said cancerous tumors can form as a result of suppressed mental stress. I don't know if the stress from Nanny's suicide caused Mum's tumor. It most likely didn't. But reading that article didn't help my relationship with my deceased grandmother.

I still wear the sweater-jacket she made me. It no longer smells like cigarette smoke or perfume. But I claim my identity as her granddaughter when I wear it. And recently I started doing watercolor. I've tried every other form, oil and acrylic, but watercolor was Nanny's. And now it's my favorite medium and I witness my genes pooling with the paint as I mix liquid with pigment and it's messy, and the lines are blurred, but when it dries, it's soft and beautiful.

That's life and faith too. Messy, blurred, and beautiful.

And even as Dad lifted Nanny's limp body from the bathtub and Mum ran to her bedroom, even as the ashes sat on the piano while Allison played "How Great Thou Art," the lines were blurred. The picture was messy.

But it hung on the walls of our hearts, unfinished. And it was home.

✴

It's hard to do a funeral for someone who didn't believe in heaven.

We sat in the front pew of Harmony St. Mark's United Church, on St. Joseph Island.

We sat, a bereaved family in nylons and button-up shirts, while Dad gave a message on salvation and grace, and he did a good job, I thought, Nanny's urn on the communion table for us to stare at.

It was a beautiful Chinese urn and Nanny would have liked it.

And for all of the ways she had hurt my mum, I wished I could tell Nanny how much I loved her.

But I know Granddad had tried, for years. And Nanny couldn't believe Granddad, and they'd ended up divorcing.

Things would have been so different, had my great-grandmother stood up to her husband from the start.

Nevertheless, she didn't. So they weren't.

Edith Pett was a mouse of a woman.

She had every right to be nervous. Her husband was terrifying. He delighted in discipline, found pleasure in making women cower, got easily disgusted.

Charles Hilton Pett was one of few who could afford electricity during the Great Depression. He was a stingy tyrant who knew how to run a business.

Then he too went bankrupt. And so did his pride.

World War II happened next, flashing across England's skies, exploding in the streets of London. Winston Churchill stood stout, a man among men, commanding justice, relieving hearts, bringing soldiers home. And then, peace.

But within the Pett household, war ensued, Charles yelling and demanding and berating his daughters and his wife, but mostly he picked on Joan, my Nanny, because she had osteomyelitis, an infection of the bones, which left marks on her skin and weakened her marrow. And most of her childhood was spent in the hospital.

Meanwhile, Joan's younger sister Shirley got to date boys and attend school and escape Charles's anger. Charles was never as mean to Shirley as he was to Joan.

Joan found solace in making music. She played the piano for hours.

Then it was pencil sketches that earned rave reviews and when she tired of those, watercolor.

Hours lost in the fine-tuning of delicate pictures, in the colorful weaving of cross-stitch, in the timeless practice of the arts.

After that came needle and cloth.

At night, flipping through fashion magazines; dog-earing a page, finding the cloth, putting eye to photo and hand to scissors and with a snip and a tuck making miracles out of material.

"A bloody marvel!" Granddad says now of the woman he married, as he leans back in his recliner and sips on a glass of water. His face beams with affection. "I say, without fear of being wrong, that NONE was superior in ability—NONE!" The emphasis couldn't be clearer. "There might be—somewhere and at some time—her equal, but I doubt it—sincerely."

Yet as Granddad knew all too well, no amount of stitching would ever mend Nanny's broken heart.

And now that broken heart sat in an urn, and my mum held her embroidered handkerchief to her mouth and it would be the most she would ever grieve.

She was a minister's wife.

She had no one to talk to, and a house to pack up.

And in 2002, she woke up with a headache that nearly killed her.

Echo Bay, Ont.
June 20, 1999

No matter how I start this, it will not be complete, for the pain of last week cannot be captured on paper. Thankfully, pain isn't permanent. Though I pray that the lessons this grief has taught me will not be in vain or forgotten.

Sunday afternoon, I walk over to Mum's at 4:00 p.m. Ring bell—no answer. Try door—locked. Ring bell—listen; no noises inside. Ernest sent to get key; I'm anxious and pray while I wait. Ernest brings wrong key—I look around windows; all blinds down; can't see in—very anxious. Ernest brings key. I go in and ask him to wait in case Mum is sick or helpless and embarrassed.

Dark—Mum not in living groom, or kitchen, or bedroom. Shower curtain across bath. Find her curled in fetal position so small and white with blood in shallow water. I know that she's dead, by suicide. Go in shock to be held by Ernest. I react by opening curtains and blinds in living room; turn on light in kitchen looking for note. Music on radio. Table arranged with envelopes. (No note.)

Go back to house and cry. Meredith hugs me. Ernest phones ambulance. We tell Allison and Meredith. Cry and hug on and off for hours. Police come and stay until 9ish. Keith doesn't get home until 8:00 p.m. I wanted him home. Told him Nanny died. Police asked gentle questions, took statement from Ernest and told us we shouldn't go into Mum's place until after coroner's report.

Don't sleep much.

9

Forgiveness

Canada: Blyth, Ontario

July 2007

> There is a God, there always has been. I see him here, in the eyes of the people in this [hospital] corridor of desperation. This is the real house of God, this is where those who have lost God will find Him. . . . There is a God, there has to be, and now I will pray, I will pray that He will forgive that I have neglected Him all of these years, forgive that I have betrayed, lied, and sinned with impunity only to turn to Him now in my hour of need. I pray that He is as merciful, benevolent, and gracious as His book says He is.
>
> Khaled Hosseini

Sometimes, Mum dances.

It happens on those days when I'm piling dishes in the sink and trying to organize the heaps of bills and coupons and Mum's pills. It happens when Mum is nodding in her chair, her afghan tucked around her legs, her tea growing cold on a tray in her lap because she can't remember how to pick up the mug. And when I have a moment, I step over and hold it to her lips and it drips down her chin and she smiles at me, the way a child would, in gratitude.

And sometimes she lays a limp hand on my arm and she tries to find the words and I just nod. Pat her hand, kiss her cheek, tuck the afghan a little tighter.

"I know, Mum," I say. "I know."

It happens then. When I decide the house is too quiet, so I turn on the CD player and Robin Mark's Celtic songs fill the living room, with its wide windows and its hanging baskets.

And I see a pink sticky note by Mum's place at the table, beside her pills and her lukewarm orange juice. The note, filled with her blue handwriting that used to be perfect penmanship, now slanted and jumbled, with prayer requests for her children.

Soon I'm helping her from the chair, and she's leaning on me because I'm taking her to the bathroom. I'm leading her, Mum's head on my shoulder, and we're in the middle of the living room when she begins to sway back and forth. She's got a smile on her face even though her eyes are closed, Robin Mark on the stereo.

> Jesus, all for Jesus,
> All I am and have and ever hope to be.

Mum is raising her hands and she's swaying and we're dancing in the middle of a holy kind of place, with laundry on the couches.

I want to be angry.

It's so much easier to be angry than it is to forgive because forgiveness means dying to those angry feelings and not acting on them. And dying is hard, but resurrection is the easiest thing because once you've died, only God can give you life. So it's not you doing it, but Jesus, and suddenly you're standing on top of a mountain seeing the world for its beauty.

I'm running, like I do every day, music in my earbuds, and it's the end of July. I've been in Blyth two months, and I'm running down the apple orchard trail. On one side of the road there's a river, a park, and the Howson & Howson flour mill. Four years ago Trent and I had our wedding photos taken in this river, standing on the stones, Trent holding me in his arms and my bridesmaids holding my dress out of the water. Now my husband is in Korea and I'm here trying to keep Mum alive.

I know Mum sees God when she's dancing. Holding her hands up to the sky, her smile says she sees him, and she's not angry. She's not angry that she can't go to the bathroom by herself or walk or talk some days, or remember simple tasks like how to press Play on the DVD player.

She becomes nothing for the way she sees God. He is her all in all. Jesus is her reality, now.

That is why worship songs and hymns make her dance. Because the music is oxygen for Mum, it's the sound of angels giving her resuscitation, and part of her is already there, in heaven, waltzing, while the other part of her can't walk here on earth.

And it's all she ever wanted to be when she grew up. A dancer.

She told me the other day, when we were sitting at the kitchen table watching hummingbirds at the feeder. She told me how she'd wanted to be a ballerina.

Mum was born in Middlesex, England, on February 15, 1956, to Joan Pett and Roy Anderson.

She had a seamstress for a mother and a police officer for a father. They lived in a little home tucked inside a village named Ashford.

Growing up, my mum knew cobblestone roads and rain clouds, tea and crumpets, crumbling old castles, green rolling countryside and thatched roofs.

British by the book, she had a lolling accent, pink cheeks, and soft blue eyes. Teatime took place every day after school and Queen Elizabeth reigned.

Ashford derived its name from two words: "ash" from the ash tree and "ford" from a river's crossing. Known for its Biddendon wine and cider, and spotted with pubs and small shops, Ashford was quaint. And Mum was quiet. She lived in England until age eleven—when her dad was transferred to London, Ontario—and hers was a simple life guarded by two close friends, Stephanie and Jane, and the protective shadow of her older brother, Peter.

And Mum danced. She showed up to ballet class, day after day, in her thick leotards, the other girls in their fancy outfits with their mothers, and her all alone because her mother preferred to stay at home and sew or paint.

And then one day the girls called her "elephant," told her she'd never be able to dance because her legs were too fat, and she ran home in her leotard, crying.

Her mother at her sewing machine, barely looking up when little Yvonne burst in and all she wanted was for her mum to see her. To tell her that she was perfect, just the way she was, to say the things a mother was supposed to say, but Joan just kept sewing and said, "Close the door, Yvonne, you're letting in a draft."

"I don't remember her ever telling me, 'I love you,'" Mum says to me.

"Who? Nanny?"

"Yes. Didn't really hug me either."

I'm running, now, and crying, music in my ears. On the other side of the road, there's a path lined with trees that leads to the apple orchard and I follow it, the rocks digging into my shoes and there's a shaft of sunlight through the leaves.

"Why, Lord?" I'm gasping. "Why did Nanny have to hurt Mum, and why do I have to forgive her, and how?"

Maybe Nanny's suicide didn't cause Mum's tumor. Maybe it

was her smoking more than a pack a day during my mother's childhood. Or maybe it had nothing to do with Nanny at all but it's always easier to blame someone, and I'm Eve that way.

And I stop in the middle of the path, heaving, my elbows on my knees. The sunlight is falling to the ground and I'm too broken to pick up the pieces.

And then I see her.

I see Nanny, in heaven, and she's laughing and twirling and she's got Mum in her arms and they're dancing. Together. In heaven.

Part of me wants to laugh.

Part of me, to cry.

So all of me just sits down in the middle of the path and waits.

I wait for forgiveness to find its place in me.

To root its deep, beautiful tendrils within the dirt of my soul because there is no justice in forgiveness. There's only grace. And grace makes way for peace.

I know I can't humanly forgive Nanny. But God can. So I ask God to give me the gift of forgiveness for Nanny.

And I unwrap that gift slowly, considering that Nanny might be in heaven, that maybe God met her in those final minutes in the bathtub just like he'd met the man dying on the cross, and said, *Today, you will be with me in Paradise*.

After a long time Peace picks me up and carries me along the running path back to Mum and Dad's house. I walk in and Mum is standing there, hands on her hips, her sweater stained from the mocha she had earlier.

"Where were you?" she says. "I've been looking everywhere."

"Just went on a run, Mum—sorry for worrying you."

She shakes her head. "You should rest, Em. I don't want you to overdo it." Then she starts humming and slowly makes her way down the stairs toward me, pulls me close.

My Nanny gave birth to this woman.

Her body gave way in labor so that my mum could take her first breath.

If it wasn't for Nanny's sacrifice, over fifty years ago, my mum wouldn't be here, and I wouldn't be, either.

Forgiving Nanny doesn't just affect my relationship with her, or with my mum, but with my own children.

We don't live for ourselves. We live for all those whom our lives touch, and I'm leaning against Mum who's holding me on one of her good days and peace wraps around us.

"Let's watch a movie," Mum says.

And we watch *Sleepless in Seattle* for the fortieth time and we laugh at all of the funny parts, as though it's the very first time, because for Mum it is.

The other day Mum was singing to Rich Mullins's "On the Verge of a Miracle."

She turned to me and said, "That's me, Emily. I'm on the verge of a miracle."

In some ways, Mum says, healing has already taken place.

And I don't believe it because I don't see it and then we go shopping.

We're sitting in a Salvation Army coffee shop, eating muffins. Mum is so tired she's leaning both elbows on the table.

We're sitting there with our bags when I say, "I sometimes wonder how God decides who to heal, Mum."

She nods, nibbles her muffin.

"I mean, we've been praying for you for four years. We've done all of the right things like anointing you with oil, renouncing past faults, you know, all of that." My face is steaming. "So what's the answer? What more can we do?"

Mum smiles. She pats my hand.

"Well the way I see it is, healing has already happened." She talks slowly, deliberately. "Look at us. We never used to be friends. And now we're very close."

She squeezes my hand and I swallow.

"There have been so many things inside of me that God has healed, Emily. So I don't know about the cancer, but he's got a plan. Sometimes it's just not what we were expecting, that's all."

Blyth, Ont.
Oct. 22, 1999

Quieter day yesterday; tired after early morning. Got regular jobs done and felt guilty about not having anywhere to go, people to visit, or work that had to be done—although there were plenty of things I could have done or people I could have visited.

Realized I'm maybe trying too hard to be liked (loved) and to find a close friend when I should be concentrating on ministering to those around me. Looking for lonely or needy people. Helping and giving, not taking all I can get. I'm way too selfish, self-oriented, self-conscious; I need to think about others more and especially keep my focus on Jesus, praying He'll guide me in all I do and say.

10

Breakup

Canada: Edmonton, Alberta

Fall 2000

> To love at all is to be vulnerable. Love anything and your heart will be wrung and possibly broken.
>
> C. S. Lewis

Trent and I dated our first year at The King's University College.

We dated while sitting next to each other in Intro to History, him getting better marks than me on his papers, written the night before, while I'd worked on mine for weeks.

We dated as I led the Mustard Seed Inner City Church team to feed street people, and Trent joined the soccer team. We dated even when I began to think maybe we shouldn't be dating anymore, when Trent started bumping into me on purpose in the university halls and it no longer felt fun. And I'd started to catch the eye of an older student.

King's was a sprawling campus in the middle of Edmonton with a student population of about 650, a step up from Mount Carmel's 40, and most of them Dutch. I fit right in with my blonde hair and blue eyes and I majored in English and minored in philosophy and I signed up for all of the clubs. I became a spiritual columnist for the paper, I led fund-raisers in the university hallways for Mozambique's flooding, I led Bible studies in the dorms, and was even part of the liturgical dance team and the snowboarding club.

And I lost interest in Trent.

We tried to make it work. He would swing by Dairy Queen where I served ice cream, after he finished shift work at a warehouse, and we'd watch movies in his basement suite and make out on the sofa. We'd joke and laugh and try to talk deep, but it felt, already, like we knew everything about each other.

Trent wasn't interested in philosophy or English. For him, life was to be lived, not questioned.

While I was intent on changing the world and discussing Macbeth, Trent was content with becoming a math teacher and playing sports, and something had to change, but it wouldn't, until the fall of 2000.

That summer, I went home to Ontario.

I lived with my parents and my brother and my sisters in a tall red brick manse beside the United Church where my dad was preaching, and I became a waitress at a restaurant in town. It was theater season in Blyth and the seniors and couples were milling in the streets, shopping and drinking coffee before their plays, purchasing leather moccasins at The Old Mill and walking the riverbanks. And the restaurant I waitressed for was owned by a dysfunctional couple who would fight in front of customers and throw pots around the kitchen. I ended up cooking for them because they didn't have enough staff and I learned how to sauté onions and stir-fry vegetables in butter.

One day, the couple went broke and I was let go. And the restaurant closed down and I sobbed on my bed for hours. Because I couldn't admit to anyone I'd lost my job, because that was failure, and we didn't fail in this family.

I cried like I used to when I was a little girl, hiccupping and unable to stop. Then my brother, Keith, came into my room, and told me it was going to be okay. He told me he was proud of me for trying and that it wasn't my fault.

This boy, born prematurely in Congo, this boy who used to sit with me in pails of water, this boy whom I'd failed to warn about the snake, this boy whose heart I'd broken when I turned anorexic.

This boy who had bought me a mug when I was in the Toronto hospital for the first time, at age eleven, at SickKids, and I didn't know he'd bought the mug, because Mum had given it to me while he'd waited outside the door.

And I'd looked at that mug, the one with the teddy bear that said, "I Love You Beary, Beary Much," and I'd yelled, "I don't want your stupid gifts!" and Keith, behind the door, hearing this. Shoving his hands deep in his pockets and scuffing at the floor while Mum told me it wasn't from her, it was from him.

I sat up that day, after Keith calmed me down, wiped my eyes after that. Went about finding myself a new job and I became a nanny for a local family the rest of the summer.

In the beginning, Trent and I talked every night before bed, the phone cord pulled down to the floor in the dining room where I lay on my stomach and he'd make me laugh, but he's much like his father on the phone. Quiet, with two-word answers. And I would have to come up with much of the conversation and eventually the distance caught up with us.

A moment of silence is conducted when something has died, to respect the loss, and I began to doubt in those moments of silence, and our relationship began to die. I began to dream again of marrying a missionary and a philosopher and a musician and it's as if all of those ideals began to fill the empty space between us. I forgot the things I loved about Trenton: his character, his farm-boy work ethic, his integrity. All I could remember was the man I'd scribbled about for years in my diary, the dreamy visionary who was much like myself.

But I also knew Trent was my only ride home.

He was driving halfway across the country to camp with my family and me in Manitoba, to pick me up and drive me back to Edmonton.

And so I decided to try to make it work, even though it wouldn't.

For years to come, my sister Allison would keep a photo of Trent and me on her bedside table, a photo taken on this camping trip in Manitoba. We are wrapped in a blanket, our hair wet from the lake water, smiling into the camera. Allison is a prophetic spirit. She sits down at the piano and she pours her prophecies into music, and she knew, the whole time we were apart, that Trent and I belonged together.

But I didn't.

We arrived at Whiteshell Provincial Park, one hundred kilometers east of Winnipeg, Manitoba, in August of 2000. The sun was setting and Trent was already there. He'd bought a new T-shirt on the drive out because he'd forgotten to pack clothes, much like he would when he flew to Thailand six years later with just his toothbrush and passport. And he was sitting on the hood of his car waiting for us, his tent set up and his handsome face full of excitement.

And I couldn't get out of the van.

Our Chrysler van with its blue flowered curtains, and I stayed in there as dusk fell and Trent's face did too. My family piling out and trying to act normal and me with folded hands in the van not sure how I felt about him. Not sure how to talk to this boy in person when I'd been doubting in private for so long.

But eventually, he came to the door, and he took my hand. "I've missed you," he said in his scratchy voice.

And I'd missed him too. I said that into the nape of his neck, which smelled of Irish Spring. My father built a fire and my sisters and brother set up the tents and Trent and I walked the beach for a while, at night, the moon like a white button in the sweater of the sky.

Over the next few days as we camped together and roasted hot dogs and he buried my sisters in the sand and chased me into the water; as we read our books by the campfire, him with his John Grisham and me with my Anne Lamott, I would try to convince myself that we could stay together and yet, when we kissed, it wasn't quite the same. All of my ideals squished between us and me wondering, *What if?*

It was the kiss of a younger couple, a couple who had met in Bible school and I was in university now, in philosophy, and life was a question. I wanted to marry a man who liked asking questions too. A man who listened to music instead of stories on tape, a man who could play the guitar with me or sing in key, a man who dreamed about doing humanitarian work.

So even as we drove back to Edmonton in a rusty red Toyota, the one Trent had traded The Beast for, and we listened to Trooper and played road games, the end was already in sight.

It didn't happen for two more months.

Because in spite of all of my doubts, Trent made me feel safe.

For the strong way he stood in his jeans and the grip of his arms around my body and the way he bowed his head and prayed over his food and over his life. I didn't think I could marry him but I was afraid of being alone.

And then, Trent told me he thought we should break up.

We were lying under a spruce tree at Capilano Park. We were talking about the future. And I was honest with him, finally, saying we were so different.

"I feel that way too," Trent told me as we lay there. "And I think we need to break up. I don't want to."

And I was crying then. Because of the way his hand felt, cupping my face.

"But I feel God saying we need to," he continued.

God knew I had been dishonest in staying with Trent. He knew I'd been acting out of fear. And Trent deserved better and Jesus thought so too.

We sat up then, and we walked to a nearby bench and we prayed about it, that Saturday in the park.

And then he took me home, and we stood just inside my door and I wanted to kiss him goodbye. I asked if I could, and we did, but then he turned, and he walked out. And I climbed the stairs to my room and sat on my bed for a very long time.

I looked at the card he'd made me, the night we'd first kissed. At his large scrawling letters across the page. I looked at the Christmas gift he'd given me that year—an ornate wooden rabbit that opened and inside, slivers of paper and on each sliver, a memory with me. Memories like "looking at the stars on the trampoline" and "playing Frisbee golf at Rundle Park."

And then I unhooked the locket that hung around my neck, the one he'd given me, and I tucked it into my sock drawer.

Trent went home, and for the next year and a half he slept with the teddy bear I had given him, and he played too many computer games, and his sister became worried about him and eventually, he moved into a bachelor pad with some friends and started dating a girl at university.

Just as I began wondering if we hadn't both made a huge mistake.

11

Prophecy

Canada: Edmonton, Alberta

Summer 2001

> Until something is prophesied, it cannot be built.
>
> Sherry K. White

It had been nearly a year since Trent and I had broken up, and the first two months I would call him, late, and ask if he would want to come over because I missed him. I missed the way he had an answer for things, and the solid way he stood his ground. I missed kissing him.

And one of those nights, we were on my bed, our clothes still mostly on but I noticed, then, how well our bodies fit together. "We're like puzzle pieces," I said to him. "Why can't we work?"

And it was the one time he didn't have an answer, and eventually I started seeing a boy named James who wanted to be a missionary and who played the guitar, and Trent and I stopped meeting at midnight.

James was short and he dressed like a skateboarder. He laughed a lot and he liked to hike and worship. We talked for hours about God and the world and we played guitar together, and once we even stayed up all night talking. That was the night we kissed and then we went to McDonald's for breakfast and from there, the farmer's market, because James liked those kinds of things, but it didn't last.

He stopped by my parents' house in Blyth the following summer and we swam together in the river, and then James said goodbye, because he was on his way to work at camp with a friend of ours from school.

A friend he'd end up marrying.

And then Greg happened, the senior philosophy student whose eye I'd caught while Trent and I were still together. He took me to a U2 concert and we talked about everything deep, like the arts and Kierkegaard, and then we kissed. Him lying on the carpet in my parents' TV room and no amount of talking or U2 concerts could make up for the way his lips weren't Trent's.

I was single for the next five months.

It was long enough for something to conceive within me, a spiritual gestation period, and I became convinced, because I'm dramatic this way, that I would be single forever. I would be a nun, and I didn't need a husband to make me happy, and I'd never really wanted a white picket fence so this was better.

And that's when I moved in with Trent's sister, Teneale.

It was January 2002. I had nowhere else to live; it was my final year of university and the family I'd been boarding with was moving.

Teneale and I had remained friends, and I'd known she was living in a basement suite by herself—the basement suite Trent used to rent, the one he and I used to date in.

So I moved in, and she met me at the door with her short blonde bob and her smiling face, and she hugged me. "I've missed you so much, Emily."

And behind her, on top of the TV, was a recent photo of Trent.

He was in a dress shirt, and he had his arms wrapped around his sisters. And he looked muscular and mature. And that's when Teneale sat me down on the couch and told me I had to get back together with her brother.

"He's found a girl, Emily," she said, "and she's very nice but she's not you." And here she started to cry. "She's not right for him. She doesn't make him smile the way you do. She doesn't make him come alive. They're too . . . similar."

I stared at Trent's sister who was so much like me, who dressed in vintage and loved Jesus and was sensitive and artistic. And I knew she was right. "But it's too late," I said. "Isn't it?"

It's so much easier to have faith on someone else's behalf, but Teneale's was enough for the both of us.

"If God wants you to be together, he'll make it happen," she said.

The next day was Sunday, and we went to church together, and across the aisle, I saw Trent standing with a boy named Mitchell from Mount Carmel who didn't have many friends. Trent was like that. He always cared for the underdog because he used to be one. In elementary he read books and liked to hang out with his family and his long legs made him awkward. It took him a while to find his momentum with a hockey stick and to hold his own on the court, but now he was the best athlete I knew. It takes time for our bodies to catch up with our minds but Trent had never lost his heart.

And during the songs, he sang with all of it, and I watched him across the aisle. And when someone asked me later how I knew Trent was the one, I said, "I knew, because I wasn't looking at his face or his body . . . I was looking inside him, and I suddenly understood what I needed in a man: someone who would be loyal to me until the end, someone who believed in truth, someone I could trust to be a good father to my children and a good husband to me."

And I went home that day and I fell on my bed and cried. For the person I'd lost. For the man that could have been my husband and my children's father.

Teneale had planned to go to Trent's that night to hang out with him and his roommates so I tagged along, twisting my long blonde hair on top of my head and doing my makeup and wearing the sweater that made my blue eyes shine.

I wore fuzzy peach perfume and when we got there, Trent was downstairs in the basement playing cards with his roommates. I wandered into his room and there, on his dresser, was a picture of him and this girl I'd heard of.

She was beautiful. And for all of my twisted-up hair and makeup I had to hold my hands to keep from throwing the picture.

In the same breath I wondered if she wasn't better for him. She wasn't as erratic or emotional, she could talk math and science with him, and maybe she would be happy just making a house for him and ironing his shirts. I didn't even own an iron.

Yet I kept hearing Teneale's voice: "She doesn't make him come alive."

We'd been apart for one and a half years. He'd loved me until a couple of months ago when he'd finally given up on me, Teneale had said, and that's when he'd met this girl, at the University of Alberta where he was getting his education degree in math and science.

Trent played cards the whole evening. I watched a movie with Teneale and then we left, and I didn't sleep that night.

I just wept and prayed God would have mercy on me, and in the morning, before school, I called home. I called Mum. Because don't we always call our mothers when life throws us down?

"Mum," I said, "did you think Trent and I were right for each other?"

She didn't hesitate. "I've always thought, and I still think, that he is the one you are supposed to marry, Emily."

When I got to school, I headed straight for the computer lab. I sat down and wrote an email to Trent that said, "I know this sounds crazy, but would you ever consider taking me back?"

It was 8:00 a.m.

I checked my email all day, between every class, and I even stayed after school, refreshing the computer screen every few minutes.

He finally wrote back at 4:00 p.m.

"Well," he wrote, "this is a surprise. I've always loved you, Emily. But I think since God confirmed that we should break up, we need to ask him if we are supposed to get back together again."

We took a week to pray about it.

I'd begun hearing from the Trinity in a way that I'd later learn was prophetic. In a way that would stop me on my way to school because I would see people for who they were.

I would see how God perceived man, and woman, and he didn't see their faces or their hands or their elbows. He saw their souls, and he gave me a glimpse of their souls like someone handing me glasses, and their souls were comprised of colors. The warmth of kindness, the cool of jealousy, the shades of anger and envy and love, and I saw these colors blending and making a person.

It was prophecy that told me God didn't want to use me for my mind but for my heart, the day my English prof encouraged me to consider becoming her intern and pursuing a master's; the same week my philosophy prof told me I should consider a master's in philosophy. And I turned them both down because of the Spirit.

And now, a couple of months later, Trent and I were praying for God to show us if we should get back together. Confirmation found me, with Bible devotions and emails from friends and family members speaking into my life. And then one day I was running, and that's normally when God meets me—something about the rhythm of my footsteps, the right-left brain, giving way to the Spirit.

And God told me in a very clear voice, as I was rounding the curve heading back to our basement suite, that Trent was the man he had prepared for me. And I argued with it, tested it.

"What will people think?" I said, because when Trent and I had first broken up, many of my friends had confirmed we weren't a good match. We disagreed a lot and we didn't have much in common, and the Spirit spoke immediately.

Don't worry about them—I'll convince them. Trent is ready. He is the man you are to marry.

We met that Friday night.

Teneale was gone with friends, and we had the basement to ourselves.

We sat awkwardly in the living room, Trent on the sunken couch and me on a chair. We laughed and then he suggested I go first.

So I did. I told him about the week, about the prophecies. About my mum. He listened and nodded.

And then it was his turn, and I asked him what he'd heard.

He smiled, the lamplight on his sideburns and his hazel eyes. He wore jeans and a shirt snug across his arms and he said, "God told me it's my choice."

I hoped I looked pretty. I hoped he remembered how our bodies fit together like puzzle pieces. I hoped I wouldn't cry if he turned me down.

And he stood up and he came to me, then, and he took my hands. "I choose you, Emily," he said. "I always have."

We knew when we got back together that it was for better or worse.

But what Trent didn't know was, back when I was single for five months, I'd signed up for a mission trip to the Middle East. I'd wanted an adventure, not a job, so I was going to graduate King's with a bachelor's in English that spring, and leave for Lebanon that fall for six months.

When Trent found out about the trip, he said he could wait for me. "I've waited this long," he said to me. "I can wait a bit longer."

I didn't know anymore. I didn't know if I should go but Trent still had one year of his education degree to complete and I'm not a quitter. And I didn't realize how long six months would be. All I knew was I didn't want to go back to school, I wasn't ready for the corporate world, and we weren't going to get married until Trent had graduated.

So I planned to leave at the end of August for Holland, and then Lebanon, to train with Operation Mobilisation International, the Christian mission organization founded by evangelist George Verwer.

And in the meantime, I went home to Trent's farm for Reading Break that February, and Marge cried when she hugged me, said she'd missed me because I was like a daughter to her.

Harvey shook my hand and we awkwardly hugged and Teshah laughed and Teneale cried.

There was coffee, and homemade cinnamon buns, and the grandmas came and they cried too, Grandma Wierenga with her white curls and her twinkling eyes and Grandma Neumann with her husband, Garth, a man with a soft heart and a loud voice who towered over us all. All of us in that extended trailer with its clean floors and its warm smells of bread and laundry. I'd forgotten how I'd fallen in love not just with a man, but with a family, and I watched Trent tease his mom and talk sports with his dad and books with his sisters.

There was hockey on the TV and Garth grunting on the couch and telling Martha to bring him something to eat and the women playing cards at the kitchen table, the same table I'd played Dutch Blitz at, years earlier.

And Teneale remembered this, too.

"Good thing we're not playing Dutch Blitz, hey Emily?"

"Oh!" I said, my face in my hands and Marge laughing. "I'm so glad you smashed that old light. I didn't like it anyway."

I looked at her. "Trent said it was an antique."

The table erupted. It had been my first visit to the farm. We'd driven out for Grandma Wierenga's eightieth birthday, attended by hundreds in the church hall.

Trent and I were calling each other Special Friends at the time. We'd gone to the house after the party was over, Marge staying at the church to clean up, and we'd sat down with Trent's sisters to play Dutch Blitz.

And I'd gotten pretty excited. At one point, my hand and body shot up as I shouted "Blitz!," smashing the light fixture and cutting my hand. Glass and blood and silence.

The girls had giggled nervously and Trent helped me clean up my hand and then we'd waited. The lights of Marge's car pulling in, and her coming in with, "Hello?"

And I'd said it through tears. "I'm so sorry, Mrs. Wierenga. I broke your antique kitchen light. I was playing Dutch Blitz and I got too excited."

She'd just thrown back her head and laughed.

"Oh honey, it's okay. I was looking for an excuse to get rid of that old thing anyway."

And here we were again, playing cards and Grandma Wierenga was winning.

And I looked around that table, the faces aglow, and in spite of everything they'd never given up on me. They'd shown me a kind of love I'd never known before, the kind that forgives seventy times seven, the kind that never stops giving.

And I wanted to marry into that love and wear it forever, like an old pair of moccasins.

12

Engaged

Canada: Blyth, Ontario

July 2002

> You've gotta dance like there's nobody watching, love like you'll never be hurt, sing like there's nobody listening, and live like it's heaven on earth.
>
> William W. Purkey

We drove out to Blyth that spring with my family, who had come out west for my graduation. I had a BA with honors, which accounted for pretty much nothing, and Trent and I were in the Toyota Tercel. It was a caravan of vehicles: my brother with his girlfriend, my parents with my sisters, and Trent and me.

And we switched seats while driving, stepping across the gears from seat to seat and it was a rush, racing my parents and my brother, stopping for picnics and KFC and camping.

We played road games and ate sunflower seeds and pretzels and we read books to each other while we rode. We sang silly songs and told jokes. We listened to AC/DC and Bruce Springsteen.

Then we got to Blyth and Trent moved in with an elderly couple named Vera and George, and I moved into my parents' basement.

Vera was half the size of George. She had a head full of soft white hair and a face full of wrinkles and her eyes were always turned up in a smile. Her shoulders were hunched over and George often had a hand on her back and he stood over her with his kind, oval, spectacled face.

We would sit in the living room on their plaid couches and drink tea. George would lean forward and ask Trent about his father's farm while Vera and I talked about the little bookstore she and George used to own in Sault Ste. Marie, just north of where we'd lived in Laird.

"You should have seen us at Christmas," she said, her cheeks pink, her hand shaking around her teacup. "I would dress up like Missus Claus and George here, he would put on a red Santa suit and we'd serve homemade apple cider all day at the store, and cookies. Oh, I wish you could have been there."

Trent slept downstairs, adjacent to the family room, which had a TV, and sometimes he and I would scour George's wall of VHS. He collected movies, and I loved to ask him for his recommendations. We would stand in George's bedroom, the four of us, because that's where the videos were, all along the wall. He especially liked the musicals and he'd hand us a stack of ten to borrow. And he'd joke about taking our money.

We both worked during the day; Trent, with pigs, at one of the largest pig farms in southern Ontario, and he always scrubbed in the shower afterwards, the pig smell in his skin. And I waitressed at another restaurant in town, the Corner Café, rolling silverware in napkins and pouring coffee and serving soft ice cream.

And every evening we'd meet and sometimes we'd make a campfire in my parents' backyard and roast wieners and we'd play Settlers of Catan with my sisters and my brother and his girlfriend.

On the weekends we'd drive to Stratford, a larger theater town, where I would one day give birth to our son, Aiden. We'd canoe down the river and picnic by the side of the bank where swans waddled, or we'd eat at a pub. We even saved our petty cash and watched *A Midsummer Night's Dream*.

And one night that summer, I surprised Trent with a midnight picnic in Vera and George's backyard. I set up a tablecloth and candles on the grass by their apple tree, and then I knocked on his bedroom window, and he crawled through in his boxers and we sat under the moon with the candles and some crackers and cheese and hot chocolate in a thermos. And we talked about our kids, our one-day kids as we always did, and what they would be like and how many we wanted and their names.

Trent wanted three.

I said I wanted four. Two boys and two girls because that just made sense, I thought.

But I didn't know then, the pain of giving birth, the way the epidural wouldn't work and my water wouldn't break, the way it would take thirty-six hours of labor, and how Trent would keep offering me ice chips and how then, finally, my body would tear so my eight-pound son could be born.

I didn't know it would take years to get pregnant, that I would share on national television how I couldn't have children and that a pastor and his wife would ask to pray for Trent and me after the program.

And I didn't tell Trent as we sat beneath the apple tree, his body so lean, that doctors had told me when I was thirteen and lying on the hospital bed, purple with hypothermia and dying, I probably wouldn't be able to have children. That I probably wouldn't get my period either, my two younger sisters already with theirs.

I'm not sure that it even crossed my mind.

I was so used to feeling normal again, after years of not. After years of copying what other people ate and following menus and wondering if I was going to balloon out because I'd had three square meals that day, I finally felt like an ordinary girl. It was the prayer I'd prayed for four years while I starved myself, as my stomach rumbled in my bed and I wrapped my fingers around my wrists and felt my ribs, and sobbed into my pillow.

And at sixteen, I'd gotten it. My period. The red tape had been cut, I was a woman, and I danced in the school halls that day.

But I'd never really dreamed of having children.

My sister Allison was born with that dream, but I wanted to be famous.

I wouldn't admit it to anyone because it sounded selfish. And maybe it made me less of a woman. All women wanted children, didn't they?

My dream was to change the world, but Trent wanted children, so while we were dating, I did too. Only he didn't know I was the babysitter who had accidentally dropped a baby.

I couldn't tell him, or maybe I wouldn't, or maybe I'd tricked myself into thinking I wanted four when really I wanted to travel the world and do things that would put my name on books.

I wanted to be a television news anchor, but when I'd told Trent that on the way home from Mount Carmel one day, he'd asked why.

"I don't know—I guess because I like to speak to people," I said. I'd always done public speaking in school, traveling to different districts and placing first or second.

"Why don't you do radio, then?" he said.

"I want my face to be on the camera."

"Why?" Trent said. We were walking side by side down the street in Capilano, our schoolbags on our shoulders, and I was suddenly very weary of the conversation.

"I guess I like to be in front of the camera; is that a bad thing?" I said.

Trent's long legs were making it impossible for me to escape him.

"Why is it so important for you to be seen? Why does that matter to you?"

It was the first time I'd been asked that. The boys in high school had always just told me I'd be good at it because I had a pretty face. I liked that answer better.

I pushed my hair behind my ear, the hair Trent called straw-gold. "I don't know," I said, my bell bottoms getting muddy in the puddles on the path. "I guess it's just important to me. I mean, don't you want people to know who you are?"

Trent laughed. His head thrown back. "I know who I am," he said. "That's all that matters. Do you know who you are?"

I didn't.

"Why do you want to become a teacher?" I shot back.

We were nearing the corner to our townhouses. "Because I love to teach," he said, "and because it makes a difference in people's lives. I can help those kids become better people. How does sharing the news on television help people?"

I hadn't thought about that.

All I wanted was to get inside my townhouse, inside my bedroom, so I could cry.

"It lets them know what's going on, and well, yeah—why are you being so unsupportive?" I said, and we were crossing the road and his townhouse was first.

I didn't kiss him goodbye that day, I just kept walking, and it wouldn't be the last time he'd ask me the hard things.

Years later, when I finally had my name on books, it wouldn't be enough, and Trent would hold me in bed as I sobbed. For the way I couldn't rest. For the way I wanted to just sit and read but always, it was writing, and painting, and trying to know who I was.

And he would take my face in his hands and he would tell me who I was: "You are loved, Emily."

But I couldn't quite believe it.

It wasn't long after the picnic in Vera and George's backyard that Trent proposed.

But he didn't propose the way he had planned.

And I didn't see it coming, that Sunday afternoon in late July.

Trent gets migraines, and this one kept him in bed, and I was over, sitting on the side of the bed, holding a washcloth to his face and a bucket to his mouth. He was throwing up and he couldn't see for the blinding pain in his temples. After a while he lay back and closed his eyes. I washed out the bucket and the cloth and then returned. He took my hand and said, "Emily—will you take care of me forever?"

I laughed. "Yes," I said.

He nodded and smiled. "It wasn't supposed to be this way," he said. "It was supposed to be in a canoe on the river in Stratford. I had it all planned but then I got sick."

He didn't have a ring. I didn't want a ring. I wanted to be unconventional, and he knew that.

But later, I'd wish for one. In Beirut in a month, the cab drivers asking me if I was single and would I please marry them and take them back to Canada? And me, longing to show them my hand, for the diamond to glint in the sun.

But a lot of things would change over the coming year.

And Trent didn't know that he was proposing to a different girl than the one he'd marry.

That I wouldn't be the same when I returned from Lebanon, and maybe it was the murder. Maybe it was the culture shock, but most likely it was the anorexia.

He wouldn't find out though, until the honeymoon.

13

Training

Holland: Debron

August 2002

> What is that feeling when you're driving away from people and they recede on the plain till you see their specks dispersing?—it's the too-huge world vaulting us, and it's good-bye. But we lean forward to the next crazy venture beneath the skies.
>
> Jack Kerouac

August in Ontario is combines in fields harvesting grain and corn and beans, the smell of shaft and root and the soil cracking from the heat. It is humid air and the Great Lakes lined with families in cottages, and long lineups at ice-cream shops.

Trent and I drove back to Alberta that month, camping along the way in each of the provinces and sleeping next to each other in separate sleeping bags. We'd read by the fire until it got too dark to see the words, then hold each other in the tent until we fell asleep, waking up early and cooking eggs and bacon over the fire.

We drove back to the farm, and a few days later Trent took me to the Edmonton International Airport, and we stood for a long time on the curb.

It would be six months before we'd see each other again. I hadn't expected to need anyone as much as I needed Trent.

But it scared me, too, this needing him. I'd grown up believing you couldn't depend on people, and so in many ways I was relieved to be going away. Even as passengers exited from vehicles and planes whirred overhead.

"You're my girl," Trent said into my hair. "Come back soon, okay?"

I nodded against his Calgary Flames T-shirt.

Smelled his skin. Wished it didn't hurt so much to be human.

I repacked when I got home. In three days I was leaving for Amsterdam for missionary training before traveling on to Beirut.

Trent called me three times the following day, in between building a calf shed with his dad. The last call, he took the phone with him (and me on the phone) on a motorcycle ride, then for a jump on the trampoline, and finally for a walk along the river. Me, listening through the receiver and him describing what he was doing with every step.

Then, at the end of our phone-date he prayed for me, words so quiet and powerful they made me cry. He prayed that Jesus would shine through me, that the Holy Spirit would give me courage, that I would pick up the language quickly, and that the Lord would provide me with a good friend.

The next day was Sunday and I was commissioned at Living Water Christian Fellowship, the church Dad had founded in the elementary school gym. When the United Church had altered its doctrine he'd started this church, with some of the original congregation behind him, and every Sunday we set up chairs and Dad's makeshift pulpit and it was the most humble and sincere church I'd ever been to.

And I hadn't been afraid until then, until the commissioning service, when Dad and the elders prayed over me, their hands resting on my shoulder blades.

I hadn't been afraid until people started asking me if I was, what with the war in Israel and Palestine, and suddenly I wondered if I should be.

But then Mum and Dad were driving me to Toronto at four in the morning, and we met up with Bethany, one of my team members, inside the international airport and I wasn't afraid anymore. I was excited. Mum looked like she was going to cry, and now that I'm a mother, I understand. Saying goodbye to your children is saying goodbye to your heart and the Middle East was not a safe place to go, but my parents trusted God more than they trusted their fears.

So Dad took a picture of Mum and me in the airport and then they left and soon the whole team was there—Canadian girls and boys heading first to London and then to Amsterdam.

In London, the connecting flight was delayed so we were put up in the Hilton for the night. I tried calling Trent because we received a free three-minute international call, but had to pass the message on to his sister, and I cried into the quilt on the queen-sized bed with its tiny bottles of shampoo and conditioner and a package of shortbread on the pillows. I wrote a note for housekeeping staff, encouraging them and telling them about Jesus, and then I fell asleep.

Holland was thatched roofs, gardens, cobblestone walks, and streams, and everywhere, biking paths.

We'd flown in that morning, August 27th, at 9:00 a.m. and had waited until 12:00 p.m. for someone to drive us to the Debron

Conference Center, two hours away. All I saw of Amsterdam was high-rises and highways, and then, we were out of the city and into lush countryside. This was where Trent's people were from. His Grandma and Papa Wierenga, and Harvey's ancestors.

Everything was peaceful and quiet at Debron, with its long, low, white buildings and thatched roofs and tables in a cobblestone courtyard. And a path that ran by the river.

There were only two of us there who were heading to Lebanon—a Korean man who didn't speak much English and myself. The rest were flying to France, Egypt, and other parts of the world, but for one week we were gathered together, worshiping outside in a theater with benches, listening to presentations on culture shock and Jesus and how to make him relevant. A young, vibrant couple named Margo and Jon did the main sessions, and during our down time I played guitar with a Dutch girl named Maaje who taught me "You Fill Up My Senses" by John Denver.

And then one afternoon we were told to go off by ourselves for a couple hours of prayer, to seek God's face and what he wanted from us during our time away.

So I took my guitar and headed to a nearby field. I sat by a fence, surrounded by long grass and wildflowers and I played and then I listened, and I journaled and I prayed.

These were my words, scrawled across the pink journal with a rose on its cover:

Abba,

Meet me here. Break open my secrets; help me to tell you what you're longing to hear. Help me to be what you want your disciples to be. Help me to hurt when I hurt you, to feel shame. Help me to stand along with you and be utterly content. To know the joy and peace of heaven.

Help me to desire heaven, and to believe in it. To make it more real than life itself.

Thank you for the many ways you encourage us. Thank you for the sunshine, the birds, the unique beauty in every place you have created. Help me to see through your eyes.

Show me how to be a missionary every day. Give me a heart for the Lebanese. Give me insight, Lord—find me worthy of wisdom. Help me to love at all times, and to never stop believing in you.

I believe I'm afraid of pain, afraid of hard things. Help me to count it a blessing when I suffer, to rejoice and laugh despite sorrow and pain.

I pray you will find no deceit in my heart.

In Jesus's name I pray,

Amen.

The grass rustling, the smell of flowers, the sun warm on my back. I heard God speak.

I have called you, he said, *to intercede for my people. They are hurting in Lebanon. I will show you their pain but not so you can take it upon yourself; only that you will intercede for them. Pray for my people.*

The next six months would be the hardest of my life. I would learn Arabic; I would experience the murder of a team member. I would teach English in a Palestinian camp to children who knew no English; I would travel by myself for miles across the Jordan and avoid the stares of men and meet with Muslim women once a week to share the gospel, and I would give my testimony in Arabic.

And I would never stop praying.

One day I would stand on a hilltop, overlooking the hills of Lebanon, and the Spirit would show me a tree, would show me a vision of myself, trying to grab fruit from that tree. And I would hear God warning me that if I didn't let go of the branch, if I didn't trust him to hold me, I would never be able to enjoy the fruit.

I didn't know then it was a warning for what I would fall into, one week before flying home to Canada. That it was a warning for the next three years of my life.

All I knew was that I was on a mission for Jesus, and that he was enough.

14

Arabic

The Middle East: Beirut, Lebanon

September 2002

> Perhaps all the dragons in our lives are princesses who are only waiting to see us act, just once, with beauty and courage. Perhaps everything that frightens us is, in its deepest essence, something helpless that wants our love.
>
> Rainer Maria Rilke

The night before I flew to Beirut I got three and a half hours of sleep and was woken at 4:00 a.m. by a man telling me the bus was leaving. I would somehow make the bus, which took us to the international airport in Amsterdam, only to wait for six hours for the plane to London.

In London I sat on the plane for one and a half hours before it took off for Beirut, next to rows of stunning Lebanese women in head coverings and their husbands who watched me. I suddenly became very conscious of my yellow hair.

And when we arrived in Beirut, there were soldiers in green uniforms with guns, and there were signs in Arabic. I applied for and received my three-month visa, and then I met a German man, Heinrich, and a Korean girl, Ae Cha. They were there to pick up Dong Sun and me, and they took us to downtown Beirut, where we ate at an ice-cream shop overlooking the Mediterranean Sea with its fishermen and its large, sculptured rocks. I drank jellab—a medicinal tasting drink with almonds in it—and was asked by all the men in the shop where I was from.

We drove into the mountains, which looked more like rolling foothills, to the village of Beittedine, to a two-story flat-roofed house with grapes crawling across its roof. Ae Cha—who would live with me—introduced me to my flatmates, her Korean friend and a woman from Canada named Sara, and they showed me around our large upper floor. Teta, an elderly Lebanese woman, lived below us and I was told that sometimes she would bang on her ceiling (our floor) with her walking stick if we were being too raucous with the worship music.

And all I could think about was crawling into bed. I'd been up for twenty-four hours.

I would remain in Beittedine for two weeks. Our team leader lived up the road from us with his British wife and their children and we would meet there regularly for meetings and prayer. Our assignment, while we were there, was to learn our way around the village and acclimate to the culture.

So I wandered the thin dusty roads with my flatmates and was introduced to women with head coverings and drab, plain dress who would stand at their doors and cry "Tfuddeli!" which means, "Come in!" and I would eat fruit and drink matte, a sweet loose-leaf tea sipped with a straw, and smile because I only knew the basics in Arabic. They would show me how to make flatbread and would ask in broken English where I was from, but it was a very poor village and not many of them knew anything but the sweeping out of the home every day and the hanging of laundry on lines and the drinking of tea with their neighbors.

I learned that the men were the religious and educated ones who met in a building down a path, while the women were kept in the dark.

One day we traveled to the cedars of Lebanon, the *ariz*, which were a lot shorter and stouter than I had imagined, then to an orphanage and to a Bedouin village that consisted of hundreds of tents in a field where nomadic families lived and grazed sheep.

I cried a lot, lonely for the familiar and frustrated with not being able to communicate. My flatmates held me and prayed over me. I listened to Arabic tapes nonstop because I was so desperate to understand what people were saying.

And one day Ae Cha sat me down. She told me that even if I didn't accomplish a single thing while I was there, that the Lord would still honor my commitment to these people. By giving up my family, friends, and fiancé, I was going to receive the kingdom of heaven.

She reminded me of humanity's ridiculously high standards and that God does not have the same standards for us. He simply wants us to love. She encouraged me to use my spiritual gifts—my big heart, she said—and to focus on getting to know the Lord.

"Six months is not very long," she said, stroking my hair. "You need to ask yourself, how do you want to return to your fiancé and family? You are going to be married in ten months—how and what of your character do you need to surrender before that? What does Jesus want of you?"

That night I walked out onto our balcony overlooking the foothills and olive groves and lemon trees and I pictured Jesus crossing those hills and I felt his heart for these people. For his people.

And it no longer felt such a task, this being here. This learning to speak a guttural language.

Because I was learning *his* language.

A language of love.

Shortly after Ae Cha spoke to me and prayed over me, I began to dream in Arabic. And by the time I left the Middle East, six months later, I was halfway to fluent.

Sometimes, when we surrender our greatest longings—such as mine, to communicate—he gives them back.

Tenfold.

15

Relapse

The Middle East: Tripoli, Beirut, and Aaley, Lebanon; Amman, Jordan

September 2002–February 2003

> The reason birds can fly and we can't is simply because they have perfect faith, for to have faith is to have wings.
>
> J. M. Barrie

Daan was like Jesus, and I was living in his house on a lumpy mattress in the guest room and there was a card on the pillow.

A card from Daan's wife, Lara, with an olive branch saying, "Welcome home."

I wasn't home. I was in Tripoli, Lebanon, and yet there was nowhere else I wanted to be. Where the Spirit is, there is freedom, and there is home in that.

Daan was Dutch, with a long, thin face and a scraggly beard and twinkling eyes and his laugh, the way he doubled over like it was the funniest thing, and sometimes a little spit appeared in the corner of his mouth.

And Nicodemus met him at night in the form of three men, sneaking out from their homes to find the missionary who biked the streets every day telling people Jesus saves.

"Come in, come in." Daan would usher with his hands and his face so close to theirs. "I'm so glad you're here." And they'd quietly step into his home.

A bare-bones home with a tired piano, leaning bookcases filled with cracked spines, and a long wooden table with benches, a teapot in the middle—always filled with matte, and the living room. A circle of mismatched furniture, and they sat there huddled for hours, over Daan's worn black leather Bible, every night.

I would watch them from the doorway of my bedroom, where I sat studying Arabic by lamplight, learning words like *khubz*, bread. I would eat fig jam on rye, and watch Daan with his spectacles pulled down his nose and his knotted finger underlining Scripture and the men just nodding.

One was a local man who owned a small store, one of thousands of stores that lined Tripoli's streets, and word had gotten out that he was learning from the preacher. And no one came to his store anymore and he had a family to provide for. His shoulders shook and Daan put a hand on him, saying, "God will provide, brother."

The other two were young boys from strict Muslim families who would be killed should they be caught.

And Daan's house would be bombed after I returned home.

There were fresh flowers in the vase on the kitchen table, and Eli, the oldest of Daan's three children, had picked them that day in a meadow near their house. A meadow surrounded by war-torn buildings.

But the flowers weren't enough. I could still smell the garbage. Everywhere, littered in the streets, and in the gutters by the apartment buildings, and children playing with it, with sticks, and skinny dogs and cats licking wrappers.

I went for a walk to the market each day with Lara, the laundry strung high across the streets like wilted flags. We bought fresh vegetables and herbs at the market, like parsley and tomatoes for tabouli, and grapes and apples. The grapes grew across the roofs of village houses, and the apples grew in orchards next to the olive groves.

Lara taught me about Lebanon as we walked, about the land of the cedars and its divided religions. She wore skirts and sweaters and her face was lined. She was a tall, thin lady, with a brisk step. She was German and spoke multiple languages and when she looked at you, she looked carefully, thoughtfully.

Traffic lights weren't obeyed, and traffic was piled. Sometimes a kid on a moped would run into a truck and the kid would fall off, and lie there stunned, and then get up and keep riding. And Lara would keep talking to me as if it hadn't just happened.

I'd arrived from Beittedine one week earlier and had been stationed there, in Tripoli, eighty-five kilometers north of Beirut along the Mediterranean coast. And I lived with Daan and Lara for two weeks, making visits with Lara to the prisons in Tripoli. Lara would take flatbread and grapes to give to the imprisoned women, and we would sing and pray, clasping their hands through the bars. I wasn't sure why all of them were there, but for many it was because of their husbands, and for others because of their faith. Tripoli was a hard place to live if you were a woman or a Christian.

And every few days I'd run across the street from Daan's house, dodging mopeds and trucks, to the restaurant to order flatbread stuffed with cheese, and it was cooked in a hole in the wall and wrapped in paper.

"These people, they're hungry for Jesus," Daan would tell me around a bite, the cheese stringing his beard, his kids around the table with their long legs, and flowers in the middle. "All we can do is love them."

They would play music sometimes on the piano, Lara on the bench, her fingers stroking the ivories and Daan laughing and raising his arms and singing, when the house wasn't full of people. And early every morning, I would catch Daan reading. His spectacles down his nose, and always the Bible.

But mostly he rode his bike, stopping for coffee with this shop owner or that, and Lara visited the markets and the prisons with me and her children in tow.

It was after the book festival that I had to leave for Beirut, to do Arabic training and then work in the Palestinian camp. It was at the book festival that Daan and his friend Saul set up a booth and gave away countless Bibles and prayed for hours with people and I sat there too, praying, and my stomach was on fire.

And I wanted to kneel at Daan's feet and learn from him, because Daan was Jesus to me. But I had to go.

So I painted him and Lara a picture, and wrote them a poem. I hugged Daan's wiry body and Lara's tall thin one and the children, and I left that low flat house in the middle of Tripoli with its garbage streets and the vase of wildflowers on the kitchen table.

The Palestinian camp was slums.

I had never seen slums before. When we lived in Africa, the houses were cement and cracked and small, but these were like children's forts. These were sheets of tin, nailed to cardboard nailed to plastic.

I stepped across bottles and waste and piles of old clothes and the alleys were narrow. A moped swerved around me with two guys on it, and they smiled at me and said, "Where you from?"

And even through the slums' windows I could see televisions and large beds in the middle of living rooms that entire families shared.

I had sweat stains by the time I reached the school and it wasn't just because I was hot. I was going to be teaching twenty-five children English, children who'd never learned any English before, and I knew about five words in Arabic, and I spent a long time cleaning off the broken blackboard and praying.

And when they filed in they were pointing and giggling and wearing blue pinafores over their clothes, and I smiled and nodded and helped them to their seats, these little five- and six-year-olds whose playground consisted of one piece of equipment on dirt.

We mangled our way through the alphabet and some songs and then they did some writing, which ended up in crumpled paper and crayons on the floor and some of the kids crying, and I was glad when it was over. But then one of the girls put her hands in mine before she left, said "Bye, Teacher," and I knew I could keep doing it for a little while longer.

And I did, taking Arabic classes in the morning and a taxi to the camp in the afternoon, and nights were spent at Rachel's apartment, the president of the Arabic school, a single missionary who watched American movies with me when I was lonely and cooked me supper.

Soon I was moving again, saying goodbye to Rachel and to those students, giving them ball caps from a business back home and them crying and me wishing I could give them more.

I packed up my suitcase and moved to the village of Aaley, a wealthy Druize village scaling the mountain, and I lived on the third floor of a house with two female missionaries, one from South Africa and the other from New Zealand.

And soon after I had moved in and started teaching English in the village school we received the phone call.

The one telling us that a member of our team, Mary Peters, had been murdered.

The day Mary died, I wrote in my journal, "How fitting that it would rain tonight. How fitting that God would cry."

The missionary team met two days later, and Mary's husband, Samuel, joined us. It was two days after the phone call, two days after Palestinian fundamentalists had burst into Mary's nursing clinic in the early hours and stuck a gun in her mouth.

Mary was a young nurse from the States who delivered Palestinian babies and every time she laid hands on the infants she'd whisper, "B'ism Yasua!" or "In the name of Jesus," and she was shot for that.

Sam walked into the room where we sat that afternoon, and he looked like a little boy with his ball cap and baggy pants, his face scruffy and everyone quiet, huddled in a circle not knowing what to say to this man whose wife had been murdered.

I said, "Hello."

Then he said, "I don't really know what to do here. I expected all of you to be on top of me with hugs and tears, but you're all just sitting there. I'll go around and hug each of you individually."

So he did.

This man, this grieving man, went around the circle, hugging us.

And after he'd done that, he sat and he ministered to us. He told us how he had been able to forgive his wife's killer immediately. "Because as soon as this happened, a seed was planted in me. And I had the choice as to whether this seed would grow into love or hatred. So right at that moment, I chose to forgive him," Sam said.

We were quiet.

"Don't wish for the strength or grace that I have," he said. "This is a gift from God. Work with the grace you have been given."

Then he shared how, as he was lying on the floor beside his wife, her blood spilled around her, her blood crying up from the ground for the people of Lebanon, spilled on their behalf, he had received a vision. He had always seen himself, before, with the sword of truth. But as he was lying there, he saw Jesus take that sword away and hand him a new one, a more powerful one.

"Satan has made a big mistake," he told us then. "If he thinks he killed both of us, he's wrong. It will be all in Mary's name that I live to evangelize. She will not have died in vain."

My Kleenex was threads in my hands. My face was swollen, and Sam shared how he and Mary had come to the Middle East as a young married couple, knowing they might die. And every day, Mary would say, "Just in case something happens, I want you to know I love you."

She and Sam had miscarried, months before she died.

Now she was one of the martyrs, singing with the angels and holding her baby.

I had a fire in my belly those six months in the Middle East because of Daan, because of Lara and Mary and Sam, and it carried me through. It carried me, alone, to Jordan, with its deserts and shepherds, with its women dressed in dark cloth, with its thick coffee, and its head scarves.

And I ate whatever the families served me, flatbread, cheese, roasted chicken, tabouli, fruit grown wild, and I interceded. I spent hours in the Wadi Rum praying, even as the camels spit on my shoes. I prayed as I waded in the Dead Sea, the salt crystalizing at my feet. I prayed as I stood at the top of Mount Nebo, like Moses, overlooking the Promised Land. And God spoke to me, even as my jeans grew snug.

But I stopped eating one week before I flew home.

I was back in Tripoli, that week, with Daan and Lara, back in the bedroom with the lumpy mattress. And I'd gone to church, the same church I'd attended those first few weeks, and one of the families invited me for lunch, for sandwiches, and even as I sat eating, their daughter told me in broken English, "You've put on weight since you came."

And I dropped my sandwich and fell hard back into anorexia.

Just days later, I flew home to plan my wedding, scribbling menus in my prayer journal, and my tears blotting the ink.

I'd failed. I'd gotten fat. I'd gotten fat on a mission trip and there was no such thing as a loving father.

There was a God in heaven who'd let me get hurt.

And there was my dad, in Blyth, who loved God and had no time for me.

They had a cake waiting for me at Living Waters, one of those sheet cakes with the thick icing. They pulled it out after church the first Sunday I was home, and I didn't eat it. It had my name on it, but I just stood and smiled while everyone lifted forks of crumbs and icing to their lips.

I wouldn't eat cake again, I'd decided. It was my new prayer. I was done praying to God. I was praying to my eating disorder now.

And there was no more fire in my belly. There was only hunger.

For all of the God I had witnessed, for all of the Bible I had seen, I couldn't find it.

Love.

It was up to me to save myself.

That February, Mum was diagnosed with a brain tumor. It was February 9, the evening of Faith and Song, the music event their church put on every year, and Mum couldn't stop throwing up.

Dad took her to emergency and that's when they found the tumor.

She'd been having headaches for weeks, and they scheduled the CT scan for March 2.

I flew home on February 28, from Beirut to Toronto.

March 2, they told Mum her tumor was growing too quickly and the surgery that had been scheduled three months from then was bumped up to March 9.

And all I could think about was getting thin in time for the wedding.

16

Washing Feet

Canada: Blyth, Ontario

August 2007

> The wound is the place where the Light enters you.
>
> Rumi

Last night I fell asleep crying. Thinking of Mum, sitting there, eating her poutine, cheese string hanging from her mouth.

We were at a restaurant with some people from church. I was at the other end of the table and couldn't reach her. I didn't want to draw attention to her, just wanted to quietly swipe at the string, make it go away. Mum sat there, letting it dangle, trying to figure out how to move her hand. How to remove the blunder. Eventually, the string fell. Landed in an orange spiral on her sweater.

She looked up at me.

"Is it tasty, Mum?" I asked.

She nodded. "Oh, yes, it's delicious."

We call them fuzzy days.

Personally I don't mind the term; it softens the harsh blow of reality. The reality of Mum's tumor. The reality of it growing 0.5 millimeters each month. The reality of her slipping through our fingers, despite desperate attempts to hold on. The reality of feeling ignored by God as the mother who gave me life enters death.

Brain cancer. Every day the words sink in as I try to stay brave for a woman who's been nothing but brave. I am trying desperately to make up for lost time, time that trickled while I chased travels and studies and boys. Ignoring my need for my mother, when all the time she needed me.

Well, I'm here now. I've dropped everything—my work, my friends, even my husband—to tend to the woman who brought me into this world, diapered me in cloth, sang me lullabies under African skies.

I'm twenty-seven and a little kid at heart, but I'm trying to be a woman. I'm putting my mother in diapers, washing behind her ears, brushing her teeth, and kneeling down to pray with her at bedtime, hoping that somehow, somewhere God is listening.

How can you love a God who strings stars in the sky yet cannot even spare a good person cancer?

How can you love a God who watches a grown woman wet her bed?

Yet for all of my angry screams into a black universe I am drawn to the light that is him.

My skin is covered in dirt.

I've been working in the garden, and somehow it started working on me.

Mum puts her hand to her cheek as I walk in. Her eyes go big. "Just a minute," she says. Patters away in her slippers to the bedroom. In a little while, she's standing there, again, holding a steaming bucket of soapy water. Looking like she's about to fall over.

"Emily," she says in a strong voice, "I'm going to wash your feet."

I start to protest, then glance down. Dirt is caked between my toes.

"Okay," I say, taking the bucket from her tight grip and following her into the family room.

She's already laid out a scrub brush, a dozen bottles of lotion, a towel, and her bright yellow ducky.

Since getting cancer, Mum loves stuffed animals. She falls asleep every night clutching a stuffy. Her yellow ducky is the latest addition. If you squeeze its wingtip, this particular duck sings, "If you're happy and you know it, clap your hands," then proceeds to jump up and down until he falls over.

Mum sits down on a stool by my feet and takes the ducky and squeezes its wing. As he sings and dances, my feet are washed and I can't help but cry as Mum's gentle hands touch my disgusting, grimy soles, massaging them in the warm fragranced water. I think of Jesus washing his disciples' feet.

The ducky dancing absurdly.

The dirt being washed away.

The next morning Mum can't distinguish between her sandwich and her cookie.

She's dressed entirely in blue; her shirt is tucked into her stretchy pants, which are pulled up so high it looks like she has no waist. She's slouched over the table when I come upstairs, staring at the peanut butter and cheese sandwich Dad made her before leaving for work.

I'm kicking myself for not waking up sooner. She doesn't seem to notice. Just smiles at me. Her left hand hanging limply at her side. I know she's spent the past hour trying to figure out how to pick up her sandwich.

"Is this breakfast?" I say. "Or lunch?"

"Yes."

"Are you hungry?"

"Oh, definitely," she says.

I gently wrap her left hand around the sandwich, help her lift it to her mouth. She eagerly chews.

I put on some music, feed her more cheese and bread.

That's when I ask if she wants a cookie.

She looks at me, then the sandwich. Points to it. "This?"

"No, this is a sandwich. Would you like a cookie?"

She looks confused, eyes vacant.

Then she picks up her yellow napkin and begins to keep time with the song on the CD. Starts to sing. "Hallelujah, Jesus is my everything."

Doesn't miss a beat.

We used to go square dancing as a family. We'd bundle into the minivan and drive to a country church tucked between pine trees and mulberry bushes. Inside, the music roused heartbeats, the stomping of cowboy boots and the swinging of partners round and round in do-si-dos and allemande lefts.

Once, inspired by the moment, Dad leaned over and kissed Mum on the cheek; she blushed and pulled away.

"Ernest!" she said. "Someone may be watching!"

Someone was watching. In fact, four people were: me, my brother, and my two sisters. Dad stammered and looked away.

First it was Africa. Then, after those two years in Congo and Nigeria—two years of not understanding the people around her nor the culture she was in, two years of watching her husband love his life while she lost hers, two years of dirt and cockroaches and parasites that embedded themselves into the laundry and then into our skin, on behalf of some "call" she never quite heard—Dad said he was meant to be a minister.

Africa changed Mum. Dad, she felt, was in some ways no different from her father—quietly dominating women, getting his way no matter what. He was stubborn in a silent kind of way. She wasn't sure if she preferred overt honesty or subtle deception. It seemed she would never have a life of her own. So she resigned herself to caring for her kids and shrinking away from a man who asked her to relocate their home every few years on account of the "call."

It wasn't that they didn't see eye to eye. Mum and Dad were very similar in their frugality, their love of God, and their global-consciousness. But Mum was alone for most of the day with us kids while Dad studied or worked. Then she got shoved into the pastor's wife role she never quite knew how to handle, a life of pretending to be something she wasn't.

Dad took care of us once a month while Mum went shopping to the Salvation Army or Value Village, and she would remind him, "Now Ernest, they're your kids too, remember? It's not just babysitting. They need to know who you are."

And he would try. But it rarely felt natural; we knew his mind was always on his books or his computer or his upcoming sermon.

This is why Mum pulled away in public from the man she married, and why I curled up inside myself and wondered what it felt like to be held.

Mum's tumor woke Dad again last night, her snoring and restless sleeping.

He is tender, broken, a vessel pouring love over Mum. He has grey hair and weathered skin, his eyes, hollow caves of sleepless nights, but ever-present, ever willing to listen, to connect.

It's nothing, now, for Mum to wrap her arms around Dad's neck and smile up at him. He smiles right back, loving her with every awkward hug and palm-press.

They spend evenings snuggled in front of the television watching movies, knees touching under an afghan. And whenever Mum is up for it, they go for walks after supper. I often stand at the kitchen window and watch as they move, one body, hands tucked into each other's, Dad with his light blue hat perched atop thinning hair, Mum with her pink one pulled snug around her ears.

They stop at a neighbor's, take the leash of a large dog named Megan, and let the dog walk them. When they arrive back home they're glowing; it's time for a snack and some funnies on the telly before Mum begins to doze on Dad's shoulder and he gently lifts her from the couch and helps her to bed.

Watch me take care of you. God's voice is a whisper as I work in the garden.

"Why do you sound like Trenton?" I say to him.

I often use the voices of people that humans trust to convey my message, he says.

What does it look like, when God takes care of you? Does it look like me sobbing into my pillow because it's one of those days when I realize I'm not strong enough to save my mother? Does it look like manuscripts rejected, paintings uninspired, birds eating the raspberries in our garden, and the brokenhearted world weeping outside my window?

Perhaps it looks like rain on dusty soil.

Like the International Justice Mission, freeing victims of injustice.

Like the tomatoes, carrots, and zucchini that weren't attacked by the birds.

Like the poem on my blog that connects me with a complete stranger across the waters.

Like my husband, who, when we're together, asks me what he can do to make me happy.

Like the mornings when Mum isn't fuzzy and wants desperately to have a cup of tea with me.

Perhaps that's what it looks like when God takes care of us.

So I take it in strides. Life.

I'm learning to wake up and anticipate moments instead of fretting over the entire day. I'm learning to relax, because if something's meant to get done, it will, and if not, it wasn't. I'm learning to live in community and to create, because for me, that makes life meaningful. We were born to create. We are creators in his image.

The world may not be perfect, but we can make it seem perfect for the people we love. Home is where the heart and heaven reside, collide, and inscribe themselves on us.

St. Joseph Island, Ont.
Aug. 31, 1988

Reading Hannah Whitall Smith's book, **The Christian's Secret of a Happy Life.** *Our task is to trust God to be working in us; to make us gradually more like Jesus. So that we don't grumble about what happens, we work with God in that we allow him to mould us. He directs our paths and if we accept his will with peace and thankfulness he will transform us into his Son's image. Therefore—I'll try not to grumble when things go wrong; when life gets difficult; when people misunderstand me or don't agree with our choices; and to be patient with the children's questions and exuberance, and let Ernest make mistakes.*

17

The Ring

Canada: Blyth, Ontario; Edmonton, Alberta

February 2003

> When you have once seen the glow of happiness on the face of a beloved person, you know that a man can have no vocation but to awaken that light on the faces surrounding him. In the depth of winter, I finally learned that within me there lay an invincible summer.
>
> Albert Camus

I flew home to Blyth on February 28, 2003.

My parents tried the package of matte I'd brought from Lebanon and smiled politely at the Argille pipe, which I'd later learn was a bong. I was too naïve to know it was a bong. I'd smoked hours of fruit tobacco on that pipe with my friends in Beirut.

And we spread fig jam on bread and for a while I pretended I was still overseas, but there was a wedding to plan and Mum had already invited the church and our relatives and it was our first big fight in a long time, that spring.

I'd drawn up a seating arrangement for the backyard because Dad was going to marry Trent and me on July 9, and I didn't know then that Mum had already been praying for a year for the weather to be nice that day. And that she'd planted gardens in the fall of yellow and white bulbs to match my color scheme.

All I knew was she was getting headaches every day, and was angrier than normal and more stubborn than I remembered. And she laid down a lot.

And the seating plan hadn't allowed for Mum's guests, because I didn't know she was also using my wedding to celebrate her twenty-fifth anniversary—which was happening that August—and she'd decided to kill two birds with one stone, she said. Using our wedding, and the big white tent we'd rented.

The day of Mum's surgery, I stayed home and packed for Edmonton because I was leaving the next day to see Trent.

My mum was having brain surgery—removing seven centimeters by five centimeters of tumor from her right frontal lobe—and I stayed home to pack.

The doctors opened her skull even as I closed my suitcase.

Mum's right frontal lobe was removed at the University Hospital in London, Ontario. The morning of her surgery there was a rainbow outside our dining room window and I didn't know but Dad took a picture of that rainbow, trusting it was God's promise to him that his wife would be okay.

And even as he sat in the waiting room; even as they cut Mum open and tried to remove the cancer that was stealing her mind, he kept remembering the rainbow. Kept begging God to save the woman he'd already lost so he might find her again. So he might prove to her how much he loved her.

They wheeled Mum on a gurney down the esophagus of the hospital, white walls and white robes and voices muttering and rooms full of people and no one wanting to be there.

The men wheeled while Mum prayed. She was wrapped like fine china in tissue and trying to tuck it tighter for the British in her.

She was a private woman. A woman who'd never gone to the bathroom with the door open, now separated by a thin gown and soon to be exposed to the world.

This exposure bothered her almost as much as the ache in her head, the tumor bulging against her temple until she'd vomited in the wastebasket that morning at the doctor's office in Wingham. There for a checkup, they'd said the tumor was growing too fast.

Then, a seizure as she was leaving, and they'd rushed her by ambulance to the hospital an hour and a half away.

She'd aged in the month since the CT scan and her house had too, dust thickening on sills and baseboards. Her plants were wilting and she was sitting, day after day, eyes closed, praying to God for my wedding, that it would go as planned, that God would shrink the tumor and give her strength to weed the flower gardens before the guests arrived.

And she prayed now, the same prayer she'd prayed since the diagnosis, the gurney wheeling, and Dad in the waiting room. "Please, God, let me live to hold my grandchildren."

Mum longed to make things right, to do right by her family, to love on her grandbabies. To have the kind of marriage she'd always wanted with her husband and to be the kind of mother she was in her prayers.

If she lived to see the morning she would do this, she decided.

And even as the gurney wheeled and nurses muttered and with white all around, Mum prayed and angels hushed her to sleep.

I flew out to Edmonton shortly after returning home from Lebanon, because I needed to remember the man I was marrying. I stopped in at the hospital to see Mum, to have my photo taken with her, her head wrapped in bloody bandages and her eyes all bruised and swollen, but my mind was on Trenton.

And Dad drove me to the airport even as he'd driven Mum

to the hospital the day before, and hardly a thank-you from me before I was off.

I still remember those escalator stairs in the Edmonton International Airport and Trent standing at the bottom holding a bouquet of yellow daisies.

Standing tall and broad in his black leather jacket with a face as eager as when he'd stood on my doorstep years earlier, the day we walked the hills behind the townhouse.

We didn't say anything at the bottom of those stairs. We just kissed. It tasted like strawberries, the kind from the garden, not the store. The ones you wait all summer to eat, and when you finally do, you remember why you waited. The berries, so soft and sweet.

And we held hands while we stood at the carousel waiting for my luggage, two nervous lovers, and we talked about the flight and about the weather and about his long hair that was gelled. And Trent kept looking at me, and telling me how beautiful I was. Me trying to suck in my stomach and hoping he wouldn't notice the weight I'd put on overseas—me leaving at 120 pounds and returning a softer 135.

Then we walked out the revolving doors to Trent's new car, a Mazda 626, and as we began to drive he unrolled the roof to let in the sun and the breeze.

And I don't know that I've ever been happier, that day on the Calgary Trail.

Mum heard angels singing but everything was a mush of dark and she stretched her eyelids wide and . . . pain.

She couldn't tell where it was coming from but then, the songs became louder and the darkness softer, and a sailboat now, taking her away.

Mum woke to Dad's face over hers, and she craned her neck and exclaimed for the pain, for the darkness and the men in white who hovered. "Where's Emily?" she said.

Dad now touching her hand and peering boy-like through wire rims, a boy who loved books, a boy who found it easy to speak at the pulpit and hard to speak in private, a boy who looked as though he'd been crying.

"Hello, sweetie," he said. "Emily flew out west today. Remember, she stopped in to say goodbye? She sends her love."

Mum began to squirm for the wrinkles in her sheets. For the way Ernest looked at her in pity and the way I wasn't there. And she began to cry, Ernest and the doctors leaning close and hushing her like she was an infant and everything was wrong. So very, very wrong.

We drove to Neerlandia a few days after I had settled into a friend's house in Edmonton—a room I would live in for the next two months.

Trent took me to the farm, the grandmas there to hug me and cry because I was safe and sound, and they'd heard about the murder and I shouldn't have gone, they said, clicking their tongues, but then they hurried me inside. Marge embraced me, offered me a cup of coffee, and Harvey, with his quiet hello and his strong handshake.

The girls were beside themselves, and we all sat and talked around the kitchen table until Trent said he needed to take me for a snowmobile ride.

So we pulled on our snowsuits and gloves and we went for a ride. Down by the creek, where Trent used to float boats as a kid, where he hoped to float boats with his kids when they were older. My stomach growling with the sound of the engine.

He didn't know that I was cutting back with every meal. Breakfast was only a banana or a bare slice of toast; lunch—a piece of bread, and supper, just a small serving of whatever was being cooked because I couldn't afford to lose control again.

Trent parked by a tree, the one he'd carved our initials in.

"Remember our tree?" he said. And he kissed me.

Then he pulled something out of his pocket and he bent on one knee.

"Emily, I know I've already proposed. And I know you said you didn't want a ring but . . ."

And I started to cry. "I do, actually," I said.

"Good," he said, and he opened the lid to a delicate white and yellow gold band wrapped around a single diamond and he slid it onto my finger.

"Do you like it?" he said.

It looked like a flower.

"It's perfect."

His eyes lit up as the sun caught gold through the branches.

18

The Wedding

Canada: Blyth, Ontario

July 2003

> There are two basic motivating forces: fear and love. When we are afraid, we pull back from life. When we are in love, we open to all that life has to offer with passion, excitement, and acceptance. We need to learn to love ourselves first, in all our glory and our imperfections. If we cannot love ourselves, we cannot fully open to our ability to love others or our potential to create.
>
> John Lennon

I don't know when I started feeling afraid.

I flew home to Blyth at the end of May to plan the rest of the wedding with Mum, half her hair missing and she had chosen a hat to wear for the wedding. But still, we weren't getting along.

Somehow we'd fight most days about something and Mum complaining about her head hurting and me not really realizing that she had cancer. That the cancer wasn't going away, that even though they'd removed the bulk of the tumor there were some active cancer cells remaining, and she'd lost her right frontal lobe. Which meant she'd lost part of her mind.

And in one year the skull of the right frontal lobe would die, and the dead bone material would begin to weep with infection, and they'd have to do another surgery to remove it.

No, all I could think about was my wedding.

I bought decorations from the Dollar Store and found a woman from our church to do the photos and other women were going to cater the supper and make a simple yellow cake. The ceremony would be outside, the aisle leading up to the trellis climbing with roses, which Mum had watered and pruned and fertilized, and there would be rose petals instead of confetti following the "I now present to you . . ."

Trent and I wanted a simple wedding and a long honeymoon. We planned to travel to the Maritimes for three weeks, to take every mode of transportation—train, boat, car, plane, and hitchhiking—while staying in a hotel, B&B, cottage, and campground—so the wedding, including the dress, cost just shy of $3,000, and the honeymoon did too.

My sisters and Trent's sisters were to be bridesmaids, and wore same-styled dresses from Fairweather of different colors, and my best friend from eighth grade, Annette, was the maid of honor.

I spoke with Annette on the phone leading up to the wedding because she was married already and I was scared. She calmed me down, and arrived from Texas a few days before the wedding to do a bridal shower and pray with me.

Over the phone she told me something I wrote in my journal: "Marriage is like prayer. You can choose to enter it in duty, and endure it as an individual, or enter it willing to lose oneself to the Spirit, thus becoming one with the heart of God."

I'd write it down but I wouldn't learn it for years to come. I wouldn't learn it until I forgave my father, and all my hurt disappeared in light of Abba's love.

And that's when my heart began to break for men, and I stopped being angry, and I was finally able to submit. Something my mother said I would never be able to do.

The day of my wedding I was orange.

I'd baked too long in the sun at Goderich beach a few days before, trying to get a tan, and the following day I'd spent shivering in bed.

Annette did my makeup in my bedroom with its yellow curtains that Mum had sewn for me when I was a teenager. Outside the curtains I could see Trent playing bocce with his groomsmen in their tuxes. Marge was mingling with the guests; she was alone. Harvey had hurt his back just weeks before the wedding, and was flat on a mattress at home.

Mum knocked on the bedroom door, kissed me and she looked so lovely. Her hair had grown back in light brown curls and she wore lilac eye shadow and a violet dress.

We had gone to the hairdresser's that morning and I'd had braids woven into my long blonde hair while the other girls put theirs in a twist. Their gowns were silk and tied around the neck; mine had an empire waist.

It was hot and sunny, and Mum's year-long prayers had been answered and the flowers were in full bloom. Vera and George were there, Vera in a white hat, clutching her purse in a wheelchair because she was too frail to walk, and the seats were full.

And I felt sick.

I stepped out of the room then, and Dad was there in a smart navy blue suit. He kissed me on the cheek and said I looked pretty and I hadn't heard that much from him before. It sounded nice. And we waited in the downstairs family room as the groomsmen filed in and the band began to play. "Canon in D," and then it was my turn. And all I could think was, *Just keep smiling, just keep smiling*, even as I made my way down the grass path to where Trent stood, under the arch.

19

Honeymoon

Canada: The Maritimes

July 2003

> So it's not gonna be easy. It's going to be really hard; we're gonna have to work at this every day, but I want to do that because I want you. I want all of you, forever, every day. You and me . . . every day.
>
> Nicholas Sparks

"Emily? Do you want to come to bed?"

The sheet lay across Trent's naked body and me standing by the bedroom door with a glass of wine, and I was still in my wedding dress.

It was hard for me to take the dress off. Not because I didn't trust Trent, but just because I didn't think he'd like what he saw.

I didn't know how to wear my own skin very comfortably, and we were virgins on our wedding night in a cottage by Lake Huron. The wine was supposed to relax me but I felt nervous and tired.

Trent smiled at me, having already finished his glass. I couldn't stall forever.

I wished I knew what I was doing. Mum had slid a book on sex under my bedroom door when I was sixteen, but I hadn't read it because I was mad at her for not opening my door and sitting down with me on the quilt and looking into my eyes and helping me cross that threshold. The birds and the bees and the way they fly.

My friend Margarita from high school had taught me most everything I knew because she had a boyfriend named Don and they practiced the birds and the bees in the library behind the bookshelves. And I read Harlequins, until one day I felt dirty and put them down.

But nothing was enough for this moment.

Nothing was enough for the way I wondered if he'd still love me when he saw all of me. The dress fallen around my ankles and him finding the places that made me sing.

I had found those places in university. And now it was my job to sing for Trent.

Funny how for so long it's so wrong to do it, and then suddenly, it's wrong if you don't.

We dimmed the lights. Trent tenderly undid my buttons for me and then I wrapped a sheet around me and went to bed and lay there before him, like a shy offering, and we kissed as we always had but this time, our skin kissed too.

But when he tried to enter me, my body wouldn't let him.

I couldn't open for him and there was blood on the sheets and tears on the pillow and I couldn't look at him, even as he stroked my back and told me it was okay. "We have our whole lives together," he said. "Let's just get some sleep and we'll try again later."

"But . . . you've waited twenty-three years . . . and now I can't even give it to you." I was sobbing. "What if I just can't do it? What if I can never give it to you?"

I'm sure Trent was muffling a laugh but he just kept stroking my back and hushing me and then he pulled me close. The sheets bunched around us like white carnations, and my wedding dress a heap on the floor where it had fallen.

The next day we stopped by Mum and Dad's because we had borrowed their van and Dad was driving us to Ontario's London International Airport where we'd fly to Moncton, New Brunswick.

Mum pulled me aside in the hall and asked how last night had gone. I told her it hadn't, and, "Mum, do you think there's a chance that I can't . . . you know, have sex?" She just smiled and suggested Vaseline and hugged me. "It gets easier," she said, and it felt so right, her telling me these things. No amount of high school friends can make up for the wisdom of a mother.

And then we were off to the airport and Dad kissing us goodbye and us, with our backpacks and long legs, headed to New Brunswick.

We became man and wife in Moncton, at Leah Jane's B&B where they gave us free champagne and chocolate strawberries.

We became one on the adult-sized bunk bed in the room, and it wasn't like the movies, but it was something. And then we talked afterwards as we lay there, about what felt good and what didn't and I thought, *This is nice*. This marriage, with all of its surrendering and entering in and communicating, with all of its patience and its rewards.

But it also made me tuck my legs to my chest as I fell asleep because I was scared of the honeymoon's end. I was afraid of when life with its white-board grocery list and sticky notes would start because I wasn't ready to be a wife. I was terrified of the term "settle down," so I just kept moving. Kept traveling. For fear I'd lose myself if I stopped.

In the morning we wandered downtown after breakfast to an antique car show and then we ate at a pub for lunch. We walked by the Petitcodiac River, after the tide had receded, and it was a chocolate river bed; squares of dark earth that looked edible. We were given free cinema passes and spent an afternoon at the theater, and the following day we traveled by bus to Hopewell Cave. The grey rocks rising like heaving bosoms, and we met up with friends who were living in the area, Nicholas and Stasha, as we toured the Flowerpot Rocks.

I'd met Stasha on a plane ride from Calgary to Toronto one Christmas during university. We'd sat together and sung Christmas carols the whole ride and at the last minute, exchanged emails and here we were, on our honeymoon, among the Hopewell Rocks in New Brunswick. The Bay of Fundy pooling at our feet.

We drove with them back to Moncton, went out for fish and chips, and then Trent and I walked back to our bed-and-breakfast. The following morning we played cards on the front step while we waited for our taxi to take us to the Greyhound. Our next destination was Charlottetown, Prince Edward Island.

Charlottetown was a quick visit. The B&B was a simple bed in a woman's home, and jam and toast for breakfast and then we were off, with our backpacks, exiting the city on foot because we planned to hitchhike across Prince Edward Island to Fox River, to the cottage we'd rented for the week.

It took hours for anyone to stop. We camped by the side of the road, red clay beneath our feet, eating trail mix and leaning against our backpacks, trying to feel as hippie as we looked, but all we wanted was to reach the other side. Finally a car pulled over and took us partway to a gas station and said they were heading to the beach but if we were still there when they returned, they'd take us the rest of the way.

We were still there, so they took us to Machon Point, which led to Fox River Cottages.

Three cottages were lined up on the cliff of Fox River, and ours was the far one. It had a screened porch, a cathedral ceiling, a view of Murray Bay and Fox River and a sun deck with a gas BBQ.

A bottle of wine was waiting for us in the cottage, and a note with instructions on where we could buy groceries at the corner store.

It was a week of canoeing, of swatting mosquitos and watching seals sleep on the rocks. Of digging clams in the sand and frying them in butter and playing poker. One afternoon we walked to the nearest town, Murray Harbor, where we got a library card at the local library and borrowed books to read on the sun deck at the cottage. We went exploring in our canoes, crossing the river to the island on the other side, and we built sandcastles on the shore.

I dyed my roots blonde while we were there, and Trent—who had never colored his brown hair before—spontaneously bleached his too.

It was a small act, him bleaching his hair, but he looked more like me when it was done. And it felt a little like we were becoming the one-person marriage told us we were.

And every night as our bodies learned the bedroom dance, we were shy and vulnerable and tender with each other. Like gardeners, running our hands over our plants, we laughed a lot and marveled over the tan lines on our skin and sometimes we made love in the middle of the day, but I never let him see me very long. Always hiding beneath the sheets. Making excuses for the flatness of my chest, the curve of my hips.

And Trent kissed me below my ear even as I hoped and prayed he'd never grow tired of me.

At the end of the week we took the Wood Islands Ferry to Cape Breton, Nova Scotia, and from there, the Marine Atlantic Ferry to Port Aux Basques, Newfoundland, and a taxi to Gros Morne National Park, the second largest national park in Atlantic Canada.

Surrounded by mountains and towering cliffs, it was raining when we got there. We camped at Gros Morne in a puddle of water and Trent made a roaring fire in the camp stove. When the sky cleared we walked, and there were waterfalls and meadows and I lay down in a patch of sun and thought I could die there, happy.

It was sleeping bags for us at night, in the cool damp of the tent, and huddling close, and come morning we took a taxi to one of the small towns, Trout Village, where the houses were stacked neatly beside each other and the air smelled thick of fish. People talked in a dialect we hardly understood, rushing their words together and they tried to get us to drink Screech and to kiss the Cod.

From there, it was a ferry back to Dartmouth, Nova Scotia, where we spread our wet camping gear across the ground at a local campground and then took the bus into Halifax.

Halifax was alive with local bands and street vendors. The evenings were long in July and we walked the streets, found a small pizza joint on the corner, and ordered slices with my first beer, a locally brewed Alexander Keith's.

It was that night that we fought, on the bus ride back into Dartmouth.

Trent said something about children.

A couple was on the bus with their kids and Trent quipped about one day bringing our kids here and traveling with them and maybe it was the beer, but I said, "What if I don't want children? Would you be okay with that?"

No, he wouldn't, but he didn't say that. His face just fell and he said, "I thought you did? I mean, not right away but . . . we talked about it when we were dating."

"I just want to enjoy being married," I said. "And I don't know if I'll ever be ready for kids—you have to change your whole life for them and I have so much I would like to do."

It was a silent ride back to the campground and then Trent left for a walk by the beach. The sun falling behind the trees as I gathered up our now-dry belongings, folding them into our bags and then sitting and waiting for my husband to return.

Families all around, and children, and nothing in me making way for the idea of a family. My heart too crowded with myself.

Eventually Trent returned and he hugged me. And we went skinny dipping that night, but we didn't make love.

The next day was the last day of our honeymoon. Trent took me out for lobster, because it was my birthday—August 1—and we dressed in my wrinkled dress and his pin-striped shirt and drank wine while we peeled the succulent meat and dipped it in melted butter.

And then we were flying back to Edmonton, to the basement suite in our friends' house where we would spend our first year. Trent to work as staff with Young Life of Canada and me, to get my teaching degree at the University of Alberta.

And I planned menus the whole flight home, what I would cook each night of the week, and I was sweating as I wrote. Because suddenly, this was real. Suddenly I was married. I was a homemaker and I didn't know how to make a home.

My mum made homes; I lived in them. And I didn't want babies and the walls were closing in on this woman named Mrs. Wierenga, even as the plane touched down in Edmonton.

20

A House

Canada: Blyth, Ontario

July 2007

> In the years of living this life of faith, I have never known God's care to fail.
>
> Brother Andrew

I am in the garden, weeding, when I hear God say he has a house for Trent and me.

We had planned to move in with our friends, Nicholas and Stasha, whom we'd visited on our honeymoon, who had also taught English in Korea just south of us in the city of Pusan. We were going to buy a place together in Toronto and do communal living and grow a big garden together and chop vegetables at the same counter. Stasha and I planned all of this one day in Korea while the boys played cards, just as quickly as we'd become friends on the flight home, years earlier.

But then I had seen Mum dying on the webcam and I'd come home.

And I know now that I can't leave her. My youngest sister, Meredith, is six hours away in Ottawa at Carleton University, and my brother and his wife and kids live there too, while Allison is in Australia at Hillsong International Leadership College. Dad has no one else.

I hate when people feel sorry for Mum. "You're so good to her," they say to me, watching me take her to the bathroom in the middle of church and feed her at potlucks. And they are well-meaning but all I say is, "She's my mum."

She gave birth to me.

She homeschooled me, sewed me outfits, cut my hair, and taught me my manners. And more than anything she tried to show me she loved me through the way she cooked.

Growing up, we ate Saturday Stew. It was a conglomeration of all of the week's leftovers in one pot, because for a few years Dad's annual salary was $12,000 and my parents hated waste. So if we didn't finish our supper, it would go into the pot and we dreaded Saturdays. Liver and onions mixed with spaghetti mixed with meatloaf.

Mum didn't want us to take our meals—the blessing of having food, and the love with which it was prepared—for granted. She made love, in the kitchen. She baked homemade bread and homemade granola. She made every meal from scratch and because I was homeschooled until grade five, she did "cultural" meals once a month in which she cooked a meal from the country we were studying. I still remember the African peanut-butter stew, the chunks of beef in the peanut sauce over rice.

My mum didn't know how to tell me she loved me in words. She wasn't a big hugger and compliments didn't come naturally. But she put oregano in the spaghetti sauce. She broiled tomatoes and cheese on top of the creamy macaroni, and she crunched up potato chips in the tuna casserole. She made homemade chocolate zucchini cake because she wanted us to be healthy, and every swirl of the spoon, every donning of the apron, every evening standing over the stove was a posture of love.

Even Saturday Stew.

Because Mum cared, not only about us but about the world's children, that we would know compassion for a world in which millions of children die every year from hunger. So she taught us to clean up our plates and to this day, I do.

The kitchen table is the heart of the home, the place where nourishment happens—both spiritual and physical. It's the place where my dad would pull out his Bible with its cracked spine after Mum's homemade meal and we'd read a passage and then bring out the basket of Christmas cards, and pray for a different family each night.

But for four years I refused my mother's love.

I stopped eating, because I decided it wasn't enough for me. I needed more, but what I didn't realize was there was no amount of loving that my mum could do that would fulfill me. I needed my Abba Father's love. So out of desperation Mum began making calorie-rich meals in order to try and save my eighty-pound body. But the rest of my family just ended up gaining weight while I sat there and said "No." No to her love. No to her desperate attempt to hold a little girl who couldn't move past her hurts.

Yes, this being here is the least I can do—this staying home and taking care of Mum—my hands covered in dirt and me, bowed low.

God says he has a house for us.

But I've looked at every place advertised in Blyth, and there is nothing in our price range except for a couple of run-downs.

"Watch me take care of you," God whispers as I kneel in the garden, and I say I will trust him.

"Show me, Lord," I say, because as much as Mum's tumor is killing her, it is making both of us cling to Jesus's robe. And I cling, desperate, as Jesus lowers himself and looks me in the eye and tells me he loves me.

That afternoon I catch a ride with a neighbor family to buy organic vegetables from a local farm.

We're talking about Trent coming home in a month and me hoping to buy a house, and the woman in the front seat turns. Tells me about a private sale in the middle of town across from the school. "You wouldn't have heard of it, because it's not listed," she says. "My brother was going to buy it but now he's changed his mind—so it's available."

I grab Dad's rusty bike the moment I get home.

It's a white bungalow on a corner lot, with two large maple trees shielding the side entrance. I peer in the windows at the large living room and kitchen, a small workshop in the back for Trent, and two small bedrooms—one for an office, the other for Trent and I.

"You did it," I say to God, standing by the laundry line, looking out across the lawn and picturing a garden, flowers, vegetables, a fire pit. "You really did it."

Three weeks later, the white bungalow is ours for $79,000.

I spend hours remodeling the place. Tearing out the brown shag carpet, stripping walls of flowery paper, a black stereo on the floor and one day, a bat in the bedroom. I lock myself in the other room and call Dad and he drives over, chases the bat out with a broom.

I paint the living room crimson and buttercup; the kitchen, cumin yellow. Our bedroom is a soft tan and the office a bright purple. Underneath the shag is hardwood. In the kitchen I pull up the linoleum and stain the plywood dark green. I stain the outside steps and buy secondhand furniture.

Our office couch comes from a roadside curb in Kitchener, Ontario.

And while I pull wallpaper and carpet, as I paint and stain, I pray over these rooms. I pray they will be a respite for Dad, a place where Mum can come and stay so Dad can have a night off, and little do I know how many nights Mum will pass out on our sofa, the seizures just taking her away, or about the evening I'll have a baby shower and Mum will attend but get fuzzy halfway through. How I'll help lay her down on my bed, how Dad will come and carry her out because she can't walk, and my friends all watching.

A few days ago, Mum tried to make me carrot cake with cream cheese icing for my birthday.

Growing up, Mum baked us our favorite cakes. This year, she insisted on doing the same. I wasn't allowed to help.

At first she cracked two eggs; then she saw a bird at the window and wandered away from the bowl for a couple of hours.

Later, she pulled out some carrots to shred, but her hands shook horribly as she tried to untie the bag and she got exhausted. Had to lie down. So I grated the carrots.

Time passed. I came upon her pulling out various bowls and ingredients from the shelves. She left more things sitting on the counter and went to write in her datebook. Eventually, Dad ended up mixing the cake because Mum still insisted I couldn't help. Dad poured it into the pans and put them in the oven—and I creamed the icing, and spread it on the cake.

At the time I thought nothing of it. But today I'm painting, the radio playing something by Pink and it hits me: this isn't normal.

My mother is sick. And she keeps getting sicker.

There's no getting better, even when we think she is.

I was visiting a friend, a week ago, when Dad and Mum went out for their walk.

Whenever Mum isn't fuzzy, she takes a walk with Dad, every evening after supper.

That night Mum was alert, spry, with bright eyes and red cheeks. She and Dad held hands and walked down the gravel road farther than they'd walked in months.

They stopped and said hello to the neighbors, then reached the top of a hill overlooking wheat and rutabaga fields.

Suddenly, Mum couldn't move another step.

Dad shook his head, scratched the back of his neck. Helped her sit down at the edge of the road in a patch of grass, took off running for home. Once there, sweaty and out of breath, the car wouldn't start—dead battery. With the van on loan to someone else, he used the garden tractor.

Driving the tractor past the same neighbors with their kids and their jungle gyms, Dad made his way to where Mum sat at the top of the hill. By the time he arrived, she was stretched out flat in the grass beside the road. Her eyes closed.

Dad lifted her, draped her arms around the steering wheel of the tractor, then climbed behind her. Drove his wife home.

It took Dad twenty minutes to get Mum from the tractor into bed. Her body slung over his arms and him pulling.

He spent the rest of the night on his computer.

Mum passed out, upstairs.

Norwich, Ont.
March 19, 1986

We need to find more ways of resting while living our everyday lives. I feel a bit guilty being here (on a retreat with Ernest) away from the children this long, just for a "rest." How can we build specific times for quietness into our days? There's always so much demanding attention or things I want to do. I need to relax (Having a bath? Going for a walk?) and take time for quiet—coming to Jesus each day for strength.

21

Losing Mum

Canada: Cap-Lumière, New Brunswick;
London, Ontario

August 2007

The quiet sense of something lost.

Alfred Tennyson

It's the middle of August and we're renting a cottage in Cap-Lumière, New Brunswick, fifty minutes from Moncton. There's a panoramic view of the ocean, a beach, a lighthouse in the distance, and a large deck with a barbecue. The whole family is here, except for Trent and Allison, and Mum is drooped over and drooling. We're all trying to hold each other's heads up.

One evening when Mum is awake, I ask her if she wants a bath.

Keith says to me, "Don't you think she'll have a bath when she wants to?"

"I was just suggesting it, Keith," I say. My face is crimson and I am shaking. "And I'm sorry, who's been taking care of her all summer?"

Mum is oblivious. She pitter-patters away to the bathroom while I grab some towels and busy myself in a corner.

Keith walks up to me, hands me a piece of chocolate. "I just thought Mum might like this to go with her bath."

I start to cry. It's hard on all of us, Mum being sick and none of us really knowing what we're doing. "That's really sweet, Keith. Thank you."

Later on, it's karaoke, and Mum crooning to "Bridge over Troubled Waters."

Outside the birds are dipping across the Atlantic.

Dad is bouncing Keith's son, Isaiah, on his knee; Mum is holding the microphone close to her mouth and singing off-key; Keith and Darcie, his wife, are holding each other on the couch, and Meredith is singing along with Mum.

This is family.

And I miss Trent so very much.

Mum looks down at her watch and she is late. Her father hates when she is late, and they are supposed to meet for fish and chips and she pulls her jacket on lopsided as she walks.

She steps fast along the hospital corridor and out the glass double-doors with the shiny windows and plants crawling green and London looks different.

She doesn't remember it being so windblown and sprawling. In London it always rains, but she needs to find the fish and chips shop before he gets angry.

And her shoelaces are untied and her appointment is finished, and Ernest should have been there by now to pick her up because they were supposed to have lunch with Roy. But he isn't, and she doesn't remember Ernest asking her to wait for him in the MRI waiting room, so she will have to find the restaurant on her own.

So she walks along the streets of London, Ontario, searching for the fish and chips shop where her dad will be waiting, and she finds herself tiring fast in her white sneakers and she wonders why Ernest isn't with her.

He is always with her.

She's had another MRI, which says the tumor is growing, only she doesn't hear that, she's too busy looking at her watch and worrying about the time. And most of the time, now, she spends her days asleep or staring out a window or telling me she loves me, over and over.

She can't pull her socks on anymore and she has to wear diapers and some days she can't walk, but if the worship music is on she will sing. Her lips will move and her toes tap, Dad or myself dragging her across the carpet to her chair.

But today she can walk, and she does, cars honking as she crosses intersections not waiting for lights and checking her watch and her shoelaces untied and her, so very tired.

And she sees a restaurant sign blinking "Fish and Chips," and it is a red-brick building not like the little shop in London but it will do, and she tries to smooth her hair with a hand that shakes and the door is heavy to open.

There is a man there with tattoos and alcohol lining the walls behind him and oh dear, she is in the wrong place but she is so very tired and could he bring her some tea?

And he looks at her as so many people do these days, as though she has lipstick on her forehead and she blinks fast and looks down and sees her shoelaces untied.

Oh dear, and could he bring her some tea?

Yes, yes, he assures her, and he leads her to a table and asks if she needs anything else. "Could you ask Emily to come home?" she says. "And can you get Ernest to pick me up? He's late. And where is my father?"

And her head hits the table as the man rushes for a phone.

The police call my dad, who finds Mum sleeping on the table of the red-brick restaurant, his grey hair messed with worry.

He'd been five minutes late to the hospital, having run an errand, and Mum had gone missing and he'd run the parking lot–wide, and he'd dialed 911 and driven his car up and down London.

And they'd received a call from a man in a restaurant saying a lady was sleeping at his table, and Dad picked her up, now, like a wilted flower, and he kissed her cheeks and carried her to the car.

Promising to never leave her again.

Staffa, Ont.

Nov. 13, 1987

I am trying to make a conscious effort to make each day count (easier said than done) as it scares me how quickly the weeks and months slip by, with nothing worthwhile accomplished—nothing of lasting value—usually just stuff that has to be done over and over again; the daily "drudge" which is very necessary to a smooth-running household but leaves one wondering if there's something missing.

22

Losing Emily

Canada: Edmonton, Alberta

October 2004

> She was a genius of sadness, immersing herself in it, separating its numerous strands, appreciating its subtle nuances. She was a prism through which sadness could be divided into its infinite spectrum.
>
> Jonathan Safran Foer

Trent was biking and it was fall, and he suddenly longed for the country.

For his mother's currant tarts and fried chicken, for the way he'd compete with his grandmother to find the first strawberry of the summer, the way he'd eat peas fresh from the pod. For the whir of the combine and the smell of wheat and the call of geese. A skein of geese, his father would tell him—a flock of geese in flight—versus a gaggle, which walks on the ground. And then Harvey would proceed to remind him about a murder of crows, a pride of lions, a congregation of alligators, and a crash of rhinos. And Trent would nod and smile at his father who collects hundreds of antlers in his shed and spends hours in a rusted truck-cab in the woods, studying deer.

There in the city, the air was crowded. Car horns and tall buildings scraping sky, the smell of exhaust and Chinese takeout, and all Trent could think about was me and the way we hadn't really made love in weeks.

He biked downtown that day, in search of a flower shop. Trent used that bike every day to get to Hardisty Junior High, just across the Capilano Bridge, where he mentored youth through Young Life.

We lived in a basement suite on a quiet corner of the city.

Our Young Life friend Shane Caldwell and his wife and daughter lived above us, and some nights, when I wasn't feeling too tired, we played Settlers together and drank tea and ate nachos.

In the beginning, when we first moved, I ate nachos too—ravenous, as if I hadn't just eaten supper—and Trent would smile at the crumbs on my lips. Not knowing that I didn't let myself eat until 5:00 p.m. each day. But now I just drank tea.

Trent found a flower shop in Capilano Mall, a shop packed tight with petals, and its owner a little man with a pipe dangling from his lips. He wrapped Gerber daisies for me, two dozen of them, to remind me of the light.

To remind me of the way I used to laugh, of how Trent could make me happy, if only I would let him.

I was the associate editor of a Christian newspaper. I had tried teacher's college for a week but then I'd quit. I wasn't meant to be a teacher. It would be one of the only things I'd never finish.

I'd worked at a coffee shop on Whyte Avenue in Edmonton, a street lined with tattoo parlors and thrift stores and bong shops, and slipped muffins to street people when the manager wasn't looking, until one day someone told me about a job opening at *Living Light News*, a nonprofit bimonthly paper.

I'd interviewed for the job, and at the end of it had asked, "By the way, is this a paid position?" and the boss had laughed and said yes, and he liked my question I guess, because he hired me.

I worked there for three years and it was during that time that things got bad.

I began skipping breakfast and then lunch and drinking twelve cups of coffee a day and counting the minutes until 5:00 p.m. when I could finally let myself eat.

By the time Trent had reached home that particular day, with the bouquet of flowers, it was 4:30 and dark.

Me, sitting on the thrift-store couch, the cushions a blood-red color and my back to him. My neck curving thin into a bandana, a bandana smudged with acrylic fingerprints. And my back was shaking.

"What's wrong?" Trent said, and he put his arms around my shoulders.

"The living room," I said, shuddering, pointing at the ivory armchair and the coffee table and the Ikea bookcase. "It's all wrong. I keep rearranging, but I can't get it right. It looks so ugly."

Trent stepped around the couch, sat beside me. Handed me the bouquet.

"I brought you flowers," he said. "I should do it more often. I'm sorry that I don't."

I kissed him on the cheek. Blew my nose on a Kleenex. "Thank you, Trent. I'll put them in a vase." I smelled the daisies and smiled, then began to sob. "I'm sorry I'm such a mess. You must think I'm crazy."

Trent just took my hand. I looked at my watch. "Five o'clock," I said. "Time for supper."

"Let me make it for you," Trent said. He would make burgers and corn on the cob, and I could rest and then eat and perhaps I would laugh again like the old days. "You go lie down, and I'll take care of it. Burgers sound okay?"

I nodded. "I'm very hungry," I said.

I grabbed a bag of marshmallows from the cupboard. "I'll paint while you cook. Thanks, babes."

Then I padded away in the slippers Grandma Neumann had knitted me, to my art room, to the easel Trent had built me, to the thick-layered canvases, painted and repainted for me not being able to afford more, and I painted large faces with vacant eyes.

Meanwhile Trent made me burgers and salad, grating carrots into the lettuce the way I liked, and slicing onions even though they hurt his eyes and boiling corn on the cob. Then he set the table and called my name, told me dinner was served.

"I made you fancy salad," he said, "just for you, babes," and I emerged from the art room with an empty marshmallow bag and white-powder lips.

I sat down at the table and looked at my plate and said, "I'm not hungry."

The meal was a silent one with only Trent eating, and eventually he pushed his plate away and said, "I can't believe you ate the whole bag of marshmallows when I told you I was making you supper. And you won't even take a bite?"

And I began to cry. "You don't understand. I was so hungry. I'm really sorry . . ."

I couldn't sleep anymore.

Not since the twelve cups of coffee and not eating all day and drinking a glass of Trent's homemade wine at night.

Trent put a small TV in our bedroom and he would hold me as we watched a show in bed because he knew that was the only way I could get to sleep. And I would doze to the sound of the voices. But no matter how quietly he tried to shut it off, it always woke me up.

So I would lie there beside him trying to get back to sleep. I would even take sleeping pills but eventually they didn't work either and I would move to the couch and read something by Ann-Marie

MacDonald or some other dark author so that Trent could get some rest.

The night of the burgers and the corn and the marshmallows, I lay on the couch stuffing my face into the pillows. But I couldn't forget the way Trent had hunched over his plate trying so hard to eat, trying so hard not to walk out the door.

How could I do that to him? How could I cause him such pain?

Wrapping my fingers around my wrists, measuring.

I was trying to become invisible again.

I cried into the couch.

When I was nine, I had realized food was a choice. Mum may have dished up my meals, but no one could force it down, and the idea became a safety net, a way to escape all of the ugly in life.

But it never really helped. I just kept getting hungrier and sadder.

Then, I started eating again in the hospital after four years of starving because I was sixty pounds at five foot four, and I didn't want to die.

But now I did.

Because I didn't know who Mrs. Wierenga was.

I had just gotten used to *Emily Dow*.

And now I had a new name and a man who lived with me, who left his boxers on the bedroom floor, who I was meant to cook for every night. An authority figure, a husband, whom the Bible said I was supposed to submit to but I wasn't going to because I wasn't going to get hurt. I wouldn't let myself because submitting meant not having control and that was the one thing Mum had. She hadn't had Dad; he was always working on his sermon or his computer, but she'd had control.

So I wasn't going to let Trent hurt me either.

But that meant I couldn't let him get close to me.

And I missed him.

I had heard him slicing those onions and carrots that evening, while I'd sat on the floor eating marshmallows, cramming them into my mouth trying to fill the empty places.

I was only going to have five, but I was too hungry and suddenly the bag was empty and the burgers ready.

And he would never forgive me.

How could he?

I would never forgive myself.

I yelled, the night Trent made me popcorn. He'd made it with butter, and he sat now, his crew-cut head in his hands and the bowl of popcorn on the coffee table.

He'd picked up a movie on the way home from work, because it was Friday—date night—and we were going to have a movie and snacks, but I was yelling now. I didn't want butter, I said.

So I made my own bowl without butter and I salted it, the salt falling to the bottom of the bowl with nothing to stick to.

Another bowl, by the door, filled with Halloween candy. Trent's sister, who lived ten minutes away, had invited us to a costume party but I didn't want to go. I never wanted to go out anymore.

I sat down beside Trent and said, "I'm sorry."

And he looked at me with worried eyes. "What's wrong, Emily?" he said. "I feel like you're slipping away from me."

I put my head on his shoulder. "I'm right here, Trent. I'm sorry. I just didn't want butter, but I shouldn't have yelled."

The sound of children's boots on the stairs and I was at the door, now, exclaiming over their costumes and it was so easy to be someone I wasn't with everyone but my husband. Every day after work I would hang out with Young Life girls and I'd laugh with them and joke, and then I'd go home and get angry at Trent.

When I returned to the couch Trent tucked me under the blanket, said, "Do you know that I love you, Emily? I love your freckles, and your blue eyes, and the way you care about others."

Then he took my hands in his. "But I'm worried about you. You're not sleeping. You won't even eat butter, and you're drinking so much coffee, and you never laugh anymore. I don't know what to do."

"I'll be okay, Trent," I said. "It's just a hard time. But things will get better."

"Perhaps this will help." He stood up and hiked up his pajama pants to his belly button and did a little dance.

"Seriously, how can you resist this?" he said, dancing with his pants hiked up and I laughed.

And he kissed me then, and for a moment, I was his, and he turned on the movie and held me close. Then I took a bite of popcorn, the sound of dry kernels between my teeth.

23

The Choice

Canada: Edmonton, Alberta

March 2006

> Once upon a time there was a boy who loved a girl, and her laughter was a question he wanted to spend his whole life answering.
>
> Nicole Krauss

Springtime, with its puddles and new leaves and lengthening shadows, but I didn't notice. I was running like I did every morning at 6:30, no matter how little sleep I'd had the night before.

And I couldn't be naked anymore without shivering and Trent couldn't hold me without shuddering, bones sticking jagged.

Our love life consisted of watching TV in bed, me leaning on him and him praying into my hair until I fell asleep. Most nights, though, I returned to the sofa.

And by three or four I'd finally drift off only to wake at 6:30 to my alarm.

I would run for half an hour, shower, and drive to *Living Light News* where I'd sit in an office and drink mugs of coffee and write about people's inspiring lives.

And Trent would make his toast and leave for work praying the whole way for his shriveled-up wife and the marriage we had, a shadow of what it used to be.

I envied the way Trent treated life so lovingly. The way he got upset when he saw me eating Cheerios for supper, not because I was eating Cheerios, but because I was eating them without strawberries.

And he would cut the berries up for me when I said I didn't have time, and he would slide them into my bowl and say, "There's always time for strawberries."

And I wanted this. I wanted to love myself this way, but how could I, when doctors had told me that I couldn't have children?

They'd told me at thirteen. They'd told me as I lay dying on the bed with sheets folded in and the room smelling of Lysol and my hair falling out in clumps. They'd told me I'd done too much damage, and I shouldn't hope to conceive.

And it hadn't mattered, this not being able to conceive, until I'd met Trent and we'd dreamed of babies while lying on the floor of my living room listening to the radio. And I'd seen his eyes: the eyes of a little boy who'd held his infant cousins longer than any other, who'd rocked them and sang to them in his off-key voice and who wanted three children of his own.

How does a girl tell a boy that she is damaged? That their love, no matter how poignant, strong, or special, can't reproduce?

And so I told him I didn't want kids and then I starved myself as punishment. For not being the woman he needed me to be. For not knowing who I was apart from my eating disorder.

It was 1989. We had just moved again, and I'd seen a bad word on the side of the grocery store wall but had no one to ask about it, and Mum didn't tell me I was beautiful and Dad was never home, so I stopped eating.

I wanted Mum to say "I love you," over and over, to give me a mirror and trace my cheeks and help me believe I was worth something, but Mum didn't know how, having never known it herself, and so I broke pastels into canvas trying to lose myself in the picture.

I was homeschooled and every morning I watched the kids walking to school in Richards Landing wearing their pink and blue backpacks, and I wanted to run with them, but my legs were too fat and no one likes a fat preacher's kid.

I had cried when I'd gone to kindergarten, so Mum had brought me home, ordered books, and vowed to teach me. That kind of thing should have told me that I was extremely loved, but I didn't feel it. Because, to me, love was words and time. So I sat down to do my Bob Jones curriculum and tried to forget.

I tried to forget the way Dad had spanked me, not knowing what I'd done wrong, only that Mum told him to because she was too angry to do it herself. It didn't hurt me anymore, not even when he used his belt, because I refused to let it.

And I carried all of this anger around inside me, like a bird in a cage, until one day the bird got loose and I stopped eating.

And it felt good, this not eating, like the ribs on my fingers, as I practiced my counting. Soon I would run on thin legs with the girls next door.

At nine, Mum let me go to school again, because doctors said maybe I was lonely.

So I went to school, to St. Joseph Island Elementary with my very own backpack, but the zipper didn't do up properly because it was secondhand and I wasn't allowed to go to English class, because the books were too risqué, and the students chased me around the playground because I ate cheese and jam sandwiches. Soon I stopped bringing sandwiches to school.

I belonged to the Library Club and made a few friends who were quiet like me, and I aced every test.

But the boys didn't crush on me, and the days were long and I was tired, so I starved harder and shrunk my words smaller, until the teachers were forced to pull down their glasses and study the prose I'd made, the winning prose, and I excelled at class and flunked recess.

I didn't think God cared. I didn't care if God cared.

All I knew was he was real and that meant hell was too, and I didn't want to go there. So I'd pray for the salvation of everyone I knew at night, and dream of cheese and jam sandwiches.

There were four o'clock shadows on the lawn and on the perfectly rototilled garden.

We'd driven to Neerlandia for Easter, and Marge and Harvey were on the deck, waiting for us. Just staring at us as we parked and exited the car.

They walked over to meet us, to help us with our bags, Marge kissing us on the cheeks and Harvey and Trent talking about the playoffs.

And we went in for coffee but I didn't want Marge's fresh cinnamon buns, no thanks, and when she insisted, I said I was tired and I needed a nap.

I slept most of the afternoon and evening, and when I emerged from the room at nine o'clock, there was a child's moon in the sky and the grandmas were eating pie and playing Wizard.

And Marge asked if she could make me something to eat. I said maybe a small salad but I could make it myself, and Marge nodded. Poured me another cup of coffee.

Trent was on the couch watching a wildlife show with Harvey, who was lying on his mattress on the floor. I ate my salad then went to join Trent. He pulled me to him.

Harvey turned off the TV and sat on the couch opposite us; Marge sat beside him.

And the grandmas gathered up their things and said goodbye.

Harvey cleared his throat, looked at me.

"Emily, we love you. We are so proud of you, and so happy to have you in our family. We have no doubt that you are the one God intended for our son."

Marge was nodding. "You balance each other so well," she said.

I looked from them to Trent then back to them.

"Thank you?" I said.

Then Marge looked at me and her eyes were wet.

"We're so scared," she said, choking.

Harvey leaned forward, hands clasped on his knees.

"We're afraid you're going to die," he said point-blank.

I was silent and Trent was holding my hand but I pulled away.

"It's just that you're so very thin," said Marge. "And we don't want to lose you. We're not sure what to do, but you are our daughter. We want you to know that we're here for you, and if there's anything you'd ever like to talk about . . ." and I was rubbing my legs and nodding.

It felt like I was twelve again, and my family was assembled in the living room and Dad had his whiteboard and his marker doing the budget and talking about how much we could spend that month because we were below the poverty line, only this was worse. They were talking about me. I was the problem they were trying to fix.

I stood up.

My throat so tight I could barely say the words. "I'm sorry."

And I walked back to the bedroom and lay down on the bed and stared up at the bear skin on the wall.

We fought on the way home, and I wondered when it would all end.

I was driving and saying I felt attacked by his family, and Trent trying to explain it was the way he'd been raised. They'd always had family meetings, he said, because his family believed communication was key. And they loved me, he said.

"Well, I'm not a child anymore." I was yelling. Outside it was dark.

And he said, quietly, "Maybe you shouldn't act like one, then."

And that was it, me turning the car into oncoming traffic and Trent reaching out and grabbing the wheel.

"What are you doing?!" He pulled the car to the side of the road.

We sat there for a long time, me with my face in my hands, sobbing.

"Emily?" Trent said, putting a hand on my shoulder. "Can you look at me?"

It took minutes, but I did, and I found kindness in the lines of his eyes, in the hazel.

"I need you to choose," he said, his voice breaking. "I can't do this anymore. I'm sorry. I thought things were getting better and now . . . it's worse than ever."

Trent paused. "I can't watch you destroy yourself. I need you to choose between me and food," he said. "Because if it's food," here he choked, "I'm out."

I shook my head. "You don't understand. I want to get better. But I'm trapped. I don't know what to do, Trent."

He leaned in then and he took my hands. "I'll help you," he said. "We'll get help. But we can't keep going like this. I'm scared. We're fighting all the time and I've done everything I can think of. I've been patient. I've waited for you to come around but you're not and I can't just stand by and watch you die."

"So you're going to leave me?"

He shook his head. "Not if you choose me."

I turned and looked out the window, at the world with its traffic and its trees and its bigness.

Then I turned back, saw a man who held my hands and waited. And I remembered. The way he'd chosen *me*, so long ago, after I'd begged him to take me back. I remembered our wedding night, Trent cradling me gently after we'd tried to make love. I remembered the hours of him holding me while I couldn't sleep.

And I said *I do* to him all over again, that day in the car, to the end again.

Till death do us part.

24

Growth

Asia: Korea; Thailand; Japan; China

August 2006–May 2007

> Why do you go away? So that you can come back. So that you can see the place you came from with new eyes and extra colors. And the people there see you differently, too. Coming back to where you started is not the same as never leaving.
>
> Terry Pratchett

We moved to Korea to start again.

And little did I know that God was using Korea to grow in me a longing for family, and a belief in home.

In July 2006, after taking our Young Life kids to Rockridge Canyon—a camp in Princeton, BC—we sold our house and our red Dodge minivan and we packed our belongings in boxes, storing them in Uncle Phil's barn in Neerlandia.

My brother was getting married in Ottawa that summer so we drove our Neon to Ontario with our hiking bags stuffed. Trent stood in the wedding, a groomsman, and Allison flew home from Australia and before the wedding we sat in the backyard of Meredith's townhouse and painted our nails.

I was skinny, still, but I was eating. An egg for breakfast, a salad for lunch and then whatever was served for supper, and it was hard because I didn't know what was normal. It was hard just like it was when I was thirteen, only I'd had nurses dishing plates up for me then and this time it was just me and Trent. And Trent stayed quiet, letting me grow, all awkward and gangly and strong, on my own.

I hadn't learned yet how desperately loved I was. And this was why I'd relapsed in the first place. Because you can't become healed, truly healed, unless you revisit the past. Unless you revisit all of those aching, pulsing places and invite God into them. And that would mean going home and I wasn't ready to go home.

My brain was still too starved to learn much of anything but one day God would show me: the key with the hearts on it, the box with the lock on it, and in that box, a single mustard seed. Because in order to have faith you first have to have love, and I didn't know yet how loved I was, by people and by God.

But I was trying. I began printing off menus and following them, and learning about nutrition. Learning that eating protein during the day helped me to sleep at night. Learning that my body knew what it needed and I just had to train myself to listen. And this was a very loving thing for me to do, trusting my body this way.

Mum wore a hat for Keith's wedding. She'd had another surgery that spring, but she looked beautiful. We did her makeup and she could talk and function normally and I thought nothing of leaving for Wonju, Korea.

Because that was what we were doing. We wanted to get away, to start over, to feel alive again. And I thought maybe this would help me to get better. Maybe it would give me time to focus on me, and Trent, and Jesus, and so Trent had quit his job at Young Life and I had resigned as editor of *Living Light News* and we moved overseas to teach English.

When we arrived in Seoul, my white shirt was stained red because wine had been free on the plane.

We took a bus from Seoul to Wonju, and by the time we arrived at a small convenience store run by an elderly Korean man who knew no English I was close to crying. I had been studying my Korean dictionary for a month by then and practiced the few words I knew and the man laughed at me, his brown skin wrinkling up. We'd been given this address by the school, Yonsei ELP, but there was no one to pick us up.

Eventually the man understood I wanted to use his phone and I called the director and she apologized profusely. Said she was sending someone right away, and so we sat outside the store with our bags in the dark.

A young woman, Chun-mi, came and took us to our temporary residence in a lodge overlooking a park. The air buzzed with cicadas and the heat was drenching.

Our apartment wasn't ready and Chun-mi told us that we couldn't sleep co-ed in the rooms. Trent looked at me then and I felt like crying again because I still wasn't sleeping well and there we were in a strange country. And he turned to Chun-mi and said, "No. We're married, and we need to stay together. I need to be with my wife."

And I'd never felt safer.

After a fitful night on a thin mattress at Yonsei University we were taken to our apartment beside the *sobongso*, or fire station. It was a word we would use more than any other over the next few months, directing taxi drivers home. "*Sobongso kajuseyo?*" (Can you take us to the fire station, please?)

The apartment had a shower but no stall so the water splashed directly onto the bathroom floor and drained into a hole. It was tiny, five feet by five. There was a kitchen with a gas stove and a rice maker, a small table with two chairs and hardwood, and a large spacious bedroom with a television. The dining area opened up to a balcony with a washing machine and a drying rack for hanging our clothes, and then there was a cubby hole above the balcony.

And in the distance, there were mountains, because the one-hundred-thousand-person town was surrounded by the Chiaksan Ridge and hiking trails. Our first trip up the ridge we were offered *pondegi*, or silk worm larvae, and they tasted like dirt.

We bought a scooter, a little red 100 CC that Trent drove on sidewalks and roads, swerving around cars because there were no traffic laws in Korea, just suggestions. And we scaled heights on that scooter, visiting temples and waterfalls.

And one day I said I wanted to try to drive it, and Trent, assuming everyone had grown up on a farm riding a motorcycle, said sure, while he was playing a computer game in the apartment. It was a Saturday, and I stepped downstairs and into the bright sun and took the scooter into the street and drove it straight into a bus.

Thankfully the bus was parked.

I pulled the scooter home and Trent tried to teach me after that but I just couldn't trust the scooter enough to lean into the turns—much like the faith I claimed to have. So Trent drove, and I held on.

We taught English at Yonsei ELP, with ten other international teachers, and we'd sit in our cubicles before class, planning lessons and marking tests and eating *kimbap*—rice, vegetables, and meat rolled up in seaweed—and we didn't start teaching until 2:00 p.m.

So every morning I'd play guitar or paint and then I started taking yoga classes downtown in the local market, on the second floor, while Trent played Ping-Pong with the *ajumas*, or elderly ladies, in the same market.

And no one spoke English at yoga. It was run by a tall, kind man who nodded at me as I fumbled around my Korean consonants, and I was forced to twist my body until I ached and I learned to stand on my head and to do one hundred crunches counting in Korean (*hana*, *tul*, *set* . . .).

In October we rode Korea's high-speed train, the KTX, south to Pusan, to visit Stasha and Nicholas. And that's when we planned to move in together, back in Canada. And we bought a turtle while we were there and we carried him home in his cage on the train to Seoul, and the bus to Wonju, and the taxi to our apartment.

His name was Squirmy.

Some days we'd let him wander around on our hardwood, just a baby with a shell, and when he flipped over on his back, I would rush to turn him over but Trent would lay a hand on my arm. "Emily, he has to learn on his own." And eventually, Squirmy did.

And some nights we'd let him crawl on our bed while we watched episodes of *Corner Gas*, drinking bottles of Hite beer and eating dried squid.

And then there were the nights we couldn't sleep for the karaoke parties our neighbors put on, upstairs, their off-key voices rank with Soju or hard Korean liquor.

It droned for hours.

And with food, I was much like our baby turtle. In the same way that he fell on his back, I'd fail to eat lunch some days, to eat what I should, and Trent just waiting and praying and me figuring it out and turning back over and keeping on walking.

"What do you love about me?" I asked Trent one night as he held me in our bed.

He was quiet, and outside the branches of the magnolia tree scratched our windows. And then he spoke quiet and slow.

"I don't love parts of you," Trent said. "I love all of you. I love everything that makes you, you . . . the good and the bad, and the only reason I would want you to change anything is for your own good. So you could be happier. But nothing you can say or do could make me love you more or less. Because I love you. All of you. Forever."

Somehow I started to trust his love, there in a foreign land. He was the only thing familiar to me and I clung to him, and his faithfulness softened me. And my eyes began to open. I began to see all of the families around me, because Korea believes in taking care of their elderly and the grandmothers and grandfathers live in tight quarters with their sons and daughters and grandchildren. I began to see all of this, and the beauty of clinging to one another, and my life was a sheet of paper being folded into an origami crane and I was beginning to believe I could fly.

I fell in love with *shabu-shabu*, a Japanese dish served in a restaurant near our house. We'd sit around the table and watch the waiter prepare it before us. Submerging a thin slice of meat or a piece of vegetable into a pot of boiling water or *dashi* (broth) made with *konbu* (kelp) and stirring it.

We'd dip the cooked meat and vegetables in *ponzu* or *goma* (sesame seed) before eating it, along with a served bowl of steaming rice. Then, once the meat and vegetables had been eaten, the leftover broth from the pot was combined and fried with the remaining rice, and that soup was eaten last.

And there was *bip-im-bap*, a rice dish served in a hot stone bowl and layered in beef and vegetables and egg, and the egg would cook as the stone bowl sizzled and I mixed in *gochujang* (chili pepper paste).

And the more I ate, the stronger I became and the better I slept and the happier I was.

Trent and I wrote notes for each other. Notes which said, "SHMILY," meaning, "See How Much I Love You."

We stuck the notes in random places and sometimes I would find Trent's chicken-scratch letters in the toilet paper, unrolling, and sometimes, in my Bible or in a box of crackers.

We scrawled it across the bottom of the grocery list and arranged pebbles in the driveway. And it became an anthem of sorts, an "I Love You" anthem, sung in the drum of the everyday.

Sometimes I would whisper it in Trent's ear as we watched a show, feet touching, and sometimes he would say it to me between the sheets, but mostly, we wrote it.

We wrote it after a fight about Trent never putting his clothes in the laundry basket and after looking through old photos of ourselves as babies, all rolls and smiles, and when we were hiking the back hills behind our *apatu* or building.

It was a way to rewrite the past three years, and every time there was a note, there was a newness born in heart, a resolution to make this marriage work.

Some weeks there were more notes than others, but there were always notes. And we giggled in bed together and we pillow-fought on the couch and we played badminton in the front yard of our building.

And I almost let myself get lost in it. This love. Here in the man who kissed my nose and played poker with me and our friends at the local German pub.

But not quite, because I was still afraid, and I would get mean some days. And Trent would hide in our bedroom playing computer games or go downtown and play roller hockey with the Koreans while I played guitar and tried to sort these feelings out. Why couldn't I just let him in?

But it wasn't about Trent. It was about my spirit crying "Abba!" It was about years of hating the church for its hypocrisy and men for the way I'd always wanted my dad to hold me and it wouldn't be until I flew home a few months later and stepped into those gaping holes from the past that something big would begin to fill them. And I would finally stop fighting.

Christmas happened in Bangkok, Thailand.

It didn't feel like Christmas, the heat like feather down, and instead of turkey and stuffing we had real-fruit smoothies and beef and rice wrapped in banana leaves. Palm trees and wildcats and motorcycles, entire families piled on, including the baby. The stench of the garbage and the whir of the *tuk-tuks* (bicycle taxis) propelled by young boys in shorts.

We took the riverboat one day down to the market, down the Chao Phraya River, and seats on the boat were reserved for monks. We took it to the Wang Lang pier, and walked to the Wang Lang Market located across from the Grand Palace. There, we bartered for clothes and watches and paintings. And then we fed pigeons. We fed them chunks of bread and we headed back down the river to sleep at the house of a missionary family we knew from Canada.

The next day we flew to Ko Samui, an island in southern Thailand, and taxied five minutes to Bo Phut Resort and Spa where we stayed in a thatched roof hut and walked lush grounds to the beach. Waiters served us mai tais on the sand and we had women massage us by stepping on our backs. I got a henna tattoo and we made a sand sculpture of a turtle in honor of Squirmy.

And even though I was eating, I was still worried about my weight. But the sun was making me golden and I loved Thai food—the curries, and all the fresh fruit.

Then we rode an elephant, lumbering through the palms and feeding him bananas.

After a week at the resort, we flew to Chiang Mai in northern Thailand. We booked a village tour and a river rafting trip, and we took our backpacks through the thick foliage of northern Thailand and met leather-skinned hill tribes tucked in tree houses and huts. They played music for us, using clappers made from bamboo, and they smiled at us with huge teeth-gaping smiles. And I was learning what it was to be happy to be alive.

It was the second Sunday in January. The sun was a curl of light in the sky, like the rim of a glass. We'd attended an English-speaking church service that morning and all the Korean families sat lined up in the pews, dressed in suits and skirts, and I hadn't stopped staring at the backs of the mothers' heads leaning close to their children.

I was at the kitchen table in our apartment in Wonju, canvas spread around me, the paints I'd brought from home and I was smearing acrylic, painting picture after picture of mother and child, mother and baby, a nucleus of maternal bonding and I was trying to emote something similar. Trying to create the longing for a child within me, because I saw it in Trent's eyes. I saw our unborn child, and he missed having a family and here we were in a country filled with family and I couldn't feel it. So I hung those pictures up on my fridge and I came home from school every day and stared at them. At the curves, at the shadows between arm and baby and I began to memorize the way it could feel to want a son or daughter.

But I didn't. Not really, not yet, and I wouldn't, until one year later, when the overwhelming desire would knock me flat in Ottawa, Ontario.

It snowed that winter in Wonju, a light dusting, and we spent many weekends in the Chiaksan mountains snowboarding, but Valentine's Day weekend was Osaka, Japan.

We flew in and out of Osaka in a heartbeat, just long enough to smell the cherry blossoms, stay in a cramped hotel, and eat octopus legs.

I remember dozens of bikes leaning against each other, waiting for someone to ride them. I remember a castle and gardens and the scent of jasmine. And I remember fast trains full of men in business suits, sleeping, and everyone looking serious or sad.

Japan was a tiny country filled with countless people, everyone walking somewhere, staring straight ahead.

The day after arriving, we took the JR Railway to Kyoto. We toured one of the prettiest temples, watched hundreds of tourists drink spring water from "holy bowls," mourned for those worshiping the Buddha, and walked the cobblestone, pottery-lined streets. We ate at a small local restaurant, where drunken men blew kisses at us. We tried spring rolls and cheese balls, and some sake and dried squid.

We stayed in a cheap, Japanese-style room downtown, where the beds rolled out and the floors were covered in bamboo.

There were still so many glimpses of sadness, so many heart-rending moments in which I wanted to help people but wasn't sure how. And I know now this was the love of God at work in me, and it always had been, ever since those days in Africa when I stood staring through the fence at our neighbors, enamored by their skin, their teeth, their languid motions. It was a love so deep and fierce it hurt to breathe and it would be the same kind of love that would fly me home that summer, to take care of a mother I'd never gotten along with. And it would be the love that would one day birth in me the sharp longing for a family.

A couple of weeks later we traveled to Beijing, China, to stay in a ritzy hotel and take a tour with Stasha and Nicholas to Tiananmen Square and a Peking duck restaurant and to the Chinese opera, which sounded like a chorus of dying cats dressed in gaudy makeup. And Stasha and I were tired and got lost on the Great Wall, trying to take a shortcut.

The wall had emerged out of the mist like a passageway to a magic kingdom. It was six thousand kilometers of stone labor, seven hundred years old.

The following day, we strolled through the courtyards of the Temple of Heaven filled with people, mothers and grandmothers and children, women doing exercises in the park, a man with a red cardinal, grandfathers playing cards.

From the temple we took a rickshaw ride through the old part of the city and paid a visit to Mrs. Woo—an elderly woman who invited us into her home and shared her painful life story with us. She had a smile that lit up her tiny living room.

On our last day, we visited the zoo. Its panda bears, lions, zebras, monkeys, and elephants were lonely and shivering.

And I was too. I knew I was too skinny, still, in China. I was losing strength again and sleep. I was the turtle, flailing on my back and Trent would just raise his eyebrows and I would see the question mark there. *Do you trust my love?* it read. And slowly I would pick up my fork and take another bite.

And the more I chose love, the more I experienced Jesus.

But sometimes I still yelled, so tired of trying to be good, and Trent just held me and Jesus was in that too. In his arms.

The more he held me and the more he whispered his love to me in the crook of night, the more I began to believe that I was made for something more. That my body could be used as a home for a child and that my heart could make room for a cradle.

And little did I know that in a few short months, I would be caring for my own Mum as though she were my child, and feeling the same protective fierceness as a mother with her newborn.

25

I'll Love You Forever

Canada: Blyth, Ontario

March 2007

When you love you wish to do things for. You wish to sacrifice for. You wish to serve.

Ernest Hemingway

Mum saw the lines around Dad's eyes, the grey of his skin and the round of his pupils. He was still wearing the same clothes as when he'd found her in London, two days ago, but then again he often wore the same pants and shirt all week.

Everything about him saved: his profession, his use of water—only one shower a week, a washcloth on other mornings—and salvaged plastic bags and moldy food.

He looked so worried and she wanted to reassure him, to tell him everything was fine, but she couldn't wrap her mind around this cancer.

Couldn't understand it, and the more she tried, the more her head pounded so she just closed her eyes and hummed.

Mothers weren't supposed to get sick, she reasoned, or die.

And she picked up a *Reader's Digest* and looked at her hand. Her right hand. A hand that had signed their registry in the middle of a wheat field near Mitchell, a hand that had soothed her babies' brows and baked bread and planted bulbs and pulled weeds and it was old looking, the kind of old that she didn't recognize for the little girl inside.

Does anyone ever feel their age?

And this same hand shook bringing tea to mouth and suddenly her mouth wouldn't cooperate and tea dribbled down her chin and she began to cry.

Dad came then, taking the mug so very capably and dabbing at Mum's mouth with a cloth napkin she had sewn years ago.

"I'm sorry, so sorry," she said, and him telling her it was going to be okay.

The tea, staining places of her robe brown.

Dad sat on the old flowered couch and he rocked his wife, back and forth, back and forth, like the Robert Munsch book in which the mother sings, *I'll love you forever*, the one he read to us when we were young.

It had been two days now since he'd seen the blues of Mum's irises.

And he stared at the family photo by the recliner. His eyes on me, the girl who used to knock on his door and ask if he needed help with his sermon, or who would wait as he prepared to leave on a visit and help him with his jacket, who would stand there in her nightgown upon his return, hoping he would tuck her into bed and sing "The Lord Is My Shepherd," and he hadn't really seen me until now.

Had just patted my bowl-cut head and he'd never really heard the voice behind it all, the voice saying, "Love me, Daddy."

Mum was moaning and clearly shouldn't be left alone. Youth group was in an hour and he was the head leader. And he didn't have anyone to ask to come over and watch Mum because he was too embarrassed to let the community know he needed help.

Dad placed Mum in her chair and covered her with an afghan and opened the fridge, stared at the empty shelves, and found a block of moldy cheese which he scraped clean and sliced up, ate with peanut butter and jam on a crust of bread with a glass of skim milk.

He'd microwaved potatoes the night before, made them each a baked potato with sour cream because that was Mum's favorite, but she hadn't woken.

She still hadn't woken, and he couldn't ask the ladies from the congregation to help, for that would make him less of a pastor, leaning on his flock that way, and the sheep shouldn't have to take care of their shepherd.

Keith was so busy these days, with two kids and a career, and Allison in Australia and Meredith at school. And he thought of me and the way I'd wanted to help him when I was little.

And he picked up the phone and dialed my number in Wonju, Korea.

I lit a candle for company, sitting there in the kitchen in Korea, staring into the monitor that was my mother hundreds of miles away. Dad had set up his computer so the webcam focused on Mum's sleeping form, the video streaming across the miles into my kitchen in Korea. My job was to watch her through cyberspace, and if anything happened—if she fell out of her chair or stopped breathing or something—I was to call Dad on his cell phone and he'd drive home from the church where he was leading youth group.

The flame from the candle rose like a murmur of black starlings, and my mother's head drooped, body slouching beneath an afghan and drool forming at her mouth.

And I longed to put a pillow beneath her cheek, to massage lotion into her dry hands—hands that had once smoothed my hair, hands that smelled of Jergen's, now cracking, her nails so long they scratched her face like an infant's.

Dad had called, and he'd sounded formal at first and then he'd coughed, stumbled over his words, asking if I was busy and if I was, not to worry.

"I'm not busy," I'd said. "What is it, Dad?"

"Is there a chance you could watch your mother for a bit over webcam while I lead youth group? If not it's okay, I mean, I can figure out something else."

"Of course."

And he'd breathed deep, a quiet gasping of thanks.

I didn't understand why my mother needed watching but then I'd turned on my computer and seen.

The frail shoulders of a woman bowed low, the ghost of a woman who once bore four children, the pale face of a woman who once glowed from long hours of spading earth and pulling weeds.

And I cried so hard the chair shook. I cried until I'd pulled every Kleenex from the box, flimsy white paper crumpling on the hardwood, and I cried until my heart was wrung out.

And I sat and watched, hand by the phone, ready to call Dad on his cell if anything were to happen and he needed to rush home, but what if he was too late? What if he didn't get to Mum in time? What if, for some reason, she tried to rise and to walk down the stairs, and she fell?

I cursed under my breath, Trent asleep in the next room because it was midnight here. I cursed as though it were the screen's fault for making my mother sick, my nutritionist mother who never smoked or drank.

It was Saturday night and the candle was vanilla and I wished my mother's head would rise and she would speak again in her soft British voice and I bartered with the screen, saying I would never disrespect Mum again.

I would never throw pans or slam doors or talk back at Mum for trying to care, for making food charts for me and begging me to eat and forcing cod liver oil.

I wouldn't be angry at Mum for spending so much time in her flower beds, and I couldn't remember why I'd ever minded in the first place.

When Dad returned and thanked me and the webcam turned off, I pulled out my Bible, the one my parents had given me for confirmation, my name engraved in gold letters, and I turned the pages until I found them.

The rose petals Mum had given me so long ago, when Seth had dumped me, dried crimson between the psalms.

A faint aroma rising from their curled edges.

26

Trenton

Canada: Toronto, Ontario

August 2007

> Let there be spaces in your togetherness, and let the winds of the heavens dance between you. . . . For only the hand of Life can contain your hearts. And stand together, yet not too near together: For the pillars of the temple stand apart, and the oak tree and the cypress grow not in each other's shadow.
>
> Kahlil Gibran

He is here.

Trent has finished up his contract and returned home from Korea. He is tanned and tall and physically here.

I pick him up from the Toronto airport the third week of August, and we drive a few miles before we pull off to the side of the road and remember each other.

"Three months is too long," Trent says into my hair.

I nod. It's midnight outside and cars are careening past on the 401.

"You are here," I say, touching my fingers to his face, and he's had a long flight, an eight-hour flight with a layover in London and soon I'm back in the driver's seat and he's asleep in the back as we make the two-hour trip home to Blyth.

Our skin remembers but our hearts forget, having been apart for so long and it's a relearning, this finding a married groove in the white bungalow.

"It's smaller than I thought," Trent says of the house I've bought us, and I want to cry. I want him to see the way I've healed it; the way my hands are splintered and stained and calloused from renovating it into home. The way I've tilled the flowerbeds. The way I've labored for hours over floor and wall.

Instead he sees the fast paint job, the bits of wallpaper beneath the paint because I couldn't pull it all off and how there's tar on the hardwood planks after pulling up the shag carpet.

"It was so much worse, before," I try to say. But then he bumps his head against the too-low entranceway and we're both stinging.

The bedrooms don't have closets. We'll hang our clothes in the pantry. "It will do," I tell him.

He nods.

And I sit on the couch in the bare living room and cry, trying to understand the waves of grief. I'm mortified, yes, but it's more than that. It's like half of my body doesn't understand the other half. It's like I've forgotten what it is to be whole, and I feel criticized for doing my best. For trying to buy us a home and make it a gift.

I had been so excited to show him—and he likes the maple trees which tower over the side entrance, and the huge corner lot with space for a garden but the house has siding that is chipped and a half-shelf basement and no room for a Ping-Pong table.

What I don't know is he's feeling like less of a man right now because his wife had to buy a house for him. And deep in his marrow, he's worried he's failed me. He feels he should have been here, to take care of me, but hurt people have sharp edges and inadequacy flings arrows.

"We're not here forever," I say.

"What if your mum never gets better?" he says, and I'm not sure what to tell him. I busy myself with the dishes and look out the screen window at the stretch of grass. At the clothes on the line, all of Trent's backpacking shirts hanging fresh and laundered.

I wish we could start over and hang our marriage on the line. Let it dry in the sun and feel the wind in its creases.

"I don't know," I say, then. "But I promise you," and here I turn, "I promise, however many years we live here, I'll dedicate the same number to being near your parents, okay? We'll take turns?"

Because I know that's his dream. To live near his mom and dad, to children who grow up on the farm hearing the geese and riding the quad and feeding the cows, and I know it's hard for him to watch me making decisions for our family right now.

"Thank you," he says. "And I'm sorry, Emily. I just wish I could have been here to help you with all of this. You did well, babes."

He takes me in his arms and a breeze blows through the kitchen window. I feel it on the back of my legs.

"Will you forgive me?" he says. "I love you. And I'm here for you, for your parents. We'll make a home here. And it will be good."

I'm crying into his shirt.

It's been so long since I've had someone to lean on.

We fly out west a few days after Trent arrives home, to spend a week on the farm. We harvest the garden. We ride on the back of Harvey's tractor and eat Marge's homemade bread and cinnamon buns and play Canadian Cricket with Teneale and Teshah. And evenings are food and games.

We sleep in each other's arms in Trent's old room with the bear skin on the wall, and we want to stay forever, here, taken care of, here.

But soon it is packing up our blue plastic tubs—the ones we've stored in Uncle Phil's shed since moving to Korea—into the old Chevy farm truck Harvey has loaned us, kissing and crying good-bye, the grandmas and the aunts and uncles and Marge and Harvey and the sisters.

And they pray us off, wave us off down the straight gravel road that leads out of Neerlandia.

We stop at the US border in Saskatchewan to eat the smoked meat sandwiches Marge made us, which we scarf down, and then we find our way back to Ontario, back to the bungalow, back to the beginning.

27

Sundays

Canada: Blyth, Ontario

August 2007

> Anybody who has survived his childhood has enough information about life to last him the rest of his days.
>
> Flannery O'Connor

It is morning but Dad is still snoring.

Mum is glad Dad is back. Earlier in the night it wasn't him, and it had been scary. The imposter said he was Ernest but he wasn't, he was the man from the movie they'd watched yesterday, or the day before that.

Anyway, he was handsome but he wasn't Ernest and she will not go to bed with anyone but her husband, that is for sure, but everything seems to be okay now. Her husband is back, and he looks so peaceful.

She doesn't want to wake him but she wants her coffee. Maybe if she lies there and prays, she'll fall back to sleep, but it is almost church time and she doesn't want Dad to miss it, but he's been so tired lately.

If only she had known, she would have changed in front of him instead of in the closet. She wouldn't have yelled, she would have kissed him in public, but they always hold hands now, so that is okay and today, she thinks, is a good day.

Maybe she should get up and make him coffee and she'll bring it to him and give him a peck on the cheek.

It takes her longer to make the coffee than she thought it would, but now the sky isn't so dark and maybe, just maybe, it is time for the world to get up too, because they are all going to be late for church. And where is her bag with her Bible and glasses?

She is done with her coffee and has managed not to spill and she is ready for church. She has her skirt on and she doesn't know if her buttons are all done up but she is too tired to care. It isn't naptime yet and if she doesn't get to church then everyone will leave.

She needs to tell them Dad is coming, but she can't wake him because he looks so young and quiet.

She is pulling on her boots and jacket and everything takes so long when you don't have someone to help you, but she is having a good day.

Her purse, there, and her hat, and she is walking outside and it is nearly fall-time and her gardens are full of dirt and bulbs and she should order more daffodils. They are such a cheerful flower.

She doesn't normally walk to church and she wishes she could pedal a bike the way Dad and her used to in university, but she seems to be getting somewhere and she wonders how far the church is?

And do they have their own building now, or are they still meeting in the school?

It is time for her nap. Or maybe her mocha. No, her nap, and maybe this is her house. And where had she been walking to, again?

She needs to sleep and this house will have her bed in it.

Mum knocks on the door and someone comes, and it isn't Dad. They look at her funny, but Mum straightens her hat and smiles politely and asks if she can go to sleep now, and they know her, somehow, but she doesn't remember how, and soon she is lying on their couch and she hopes Dad will make it to church on time.

Every day is Sunday for Mum, and it takes hours to convince her otherwise, her blue bag always packed with her Bible, ready by the door.

Many mornings find her half-dressed in skirt and shirt unbuttoned and saying there are just minutes before church starts and me showing Mum the calendar. "See, Mum, it's only Tuesday." But Mum just shakes her head and asks for help with her earrings.

And when Sunday actually comes and Trent and I meet her and Dad across the road at the school gym, where we set up the chairs and pulpit, Mum's head is often drooped and I know she won't remember.

On the rare Sunday when she is awake, Mum's sore arms stretch high in worship, as if to touch heaven, and she praises the service through, me sitting beside her on a folding chair, staring at this woman with apple-red cheeks and forget-me-not eyes, the one who loves God harder than anyone around her.

Up front, at his wobbly pulpit, Dad is a humble man, wearing the same worn dress pants and button-up shirt and his hair combed across the bald spot and his eyes not quite as tired as they used to be.

He speaks of Jesus the same as before, but I hear him differently, now.

I hear the voice of a man whose wife has brain cancer. The voice of a man who spends hours massaging lotion into his wife's feet and clipping her toenails and wiping her bottom and washing her in the tub.

I hear the voice of a man who finished baking the granola his wife started making yesterday; who spoon-feeds her, who tucks afghan after afghan and pillow after pillow, who watches the same movies month after month for her not remembering.

And it is a voice that, in spite of all of this, still bows low every morning to pray; it is a voice that still leads family devotions around the supper table when Trent and I come to visit; it is a voice that still proclaims God faithful and good from the pulpit, in spite of his wife asleep in her wheelchair.

And I cry about it at night, and Trent holds me.

"I don't understand," I tell him. "I don't get it. How can Dad still believe, after all of this? So many years, I thought his faith was just routine. Dad said he believed but it was all so legalistic. No heart, just the same rote procedure—prayer for an hour each morning, and then visiting people, and writing sermons, just do, do, do . . ."

Trent waits, and listens, in our bed in the room that has no closet.

"I went to Bible school hoping to find answers and I didn't," I say. "Answers for why God lets bad things happen and all I found was more talk . . . just talk. And there's nothing worse than a mother dying but now, suddenly, all I can find is God."

I'm wearing an old T-shirt of Trent's, a Strongbad shirt, and he traces the dip of my waist as I lean on my side.

And then he prays with me for Mum, as he always does. And he kisses me. Kisses my tears, one by one, and I lean into him, the moon casting shadows on the floor.

Staffa, Ont.

Dec. 5, 1987

I grumble at God and wonder if He loves me, just because things don't go right. If everything always went right I'd have no sympathy for those who suffered and I'd have no excuse for not being joyful all the time—but I bet I'd still grumble. This way it's a test of character and faith, to see how I react to disappointments, crying kids, sickness, disturbed nights, etc.

28

Shooting Stars

Canada: Blyth, Ontario

September 2007

> Those who believe they believe in God, but without passion in the heart, without anguish of mind, without uncertainty, without doubt, and even at times without despair, believe only in the idea of God, and not in God himself.
>
> Madeleine L'Engle

It's late September, and Mum is wrapped in her afghan.

She sits at the kitchen table, reading, and I'm painting at an easel nearby.

We share a bowl of sliced apples.

There is silence save for the flip, flip of pages turning and the scratch of brush against canvas. It is a comfortable silence—like a bowl of chicken soup.

Eventually Mum says, "I love my mochas." She picks up her mug and drinks, sets it down.

"I think I like them even more than I enjoy books," she says, thoughtfully. "In fact, I'd be hard-pressed to choose if someone asked me to decide between a mocha and a book."

For a while she dozes, the book slipping from her hand. Then I step on a creaky part of the floor.

Mum's head lifts. "Mochas are supposed to be caffeinated," she says, "but for me they're quite soporific."

My paintbrush slows. I turn. "Soporific? I don't know that word."

"I learned it when I was in grade school through Beatrix Potter's books," says Mum. "It means, to mellow. To make quiet. Sleepy."

Soon, she is asleep again, her book falling to the floor.

That night we watch *You've Got Mail*, Dad at a meeting and Trent playing a computer game.

We're sitting with our feet up, hands in a bowl of popcorn.

Tonight in the middle of the movie, the part where Meg Ryan talks about bouquets of sharpened pencils, Mum turns and tells me about Dad, how they met in calculus class at the University of Guelph years ago.

"He was a bit of a nerd, you know," Mum says, her eyes shining. "He wore these huge plastic glasses and he'd push them up when he was nervous and it was very cute."

She pauses and tries to find the words, and then she says, "He's so good to me." A shaky hand now, trying to get popcorn to her mouth. "I hope he doesn't get tired of me."

I guide Mum's hand to her mouth.

And Mum's head is falling, hand back in the bowl and cancer steals her for the night.

Even as she's slouched on the couch, me sitting next to her, Mum's mind is somewhere else. She slips from present to past, remembering herself as a little girl in England and she is eight again and crying.

She pictures Nanny at her sewing machine, the thread and the cloth like love beneath her fingers and Mum wishing Nanny would touch her daughter like she did her cloth.

And she can see her brother, Peter, telling her it will be okay but he has to say that because he is her older brother and she still has her leotard on and she'll always remember this day: the day the girls called her elephant.

Her knee is torn, bloody from where she fell running home through the park away from the rehearsal, away from the skinny girls and their shiny shoes and their mothers who watched them dance.

She is a mess with too many teddy bears and she makes a fort that evening, the stuffed animals guarding her bed and she reads Jane Austen and pretends away the sounds of her parents fighting.

Then, little Yvonne sees her father at her bedroom door, holding a plate of bangers and mash, her favorite, and he uses her nickname. "Poppet—you should eat something," but she turns away. "I'm not hungry," and he kisses her forehead, leaves the sausages and cheesy mashed potatoes on the dresser and she is hungry, so she eats it, the blanket hiding her elephant legs.

She will never dance again, so she might as well eat.

She hides the plate beneath her bed and pulls the string to turn off the bulb that dangles from the ceiling.

She watches herself as a little girl, falling asleep to the sound of classical music from the living room, and there, in her sleep, her mother is clapping and the girls are standing, mouths open, as she pirouettes around them, so fast their tutus fly off, left standing in their long underwear and shiny shoes.

St. Joseph Island, Ont.
July 11, 1988

If I could be anyone besides myself, I'd be someone who was raised in a family with lots of kids, living in the country, barely making ends meet but having believing, joyful parents.

29

Sisters

Australia: Sydney

October 2007

> Sweet, crazy conversations full of half sentences, daydreams and misunderstandings more thrilling than understanding could ever be.
>
> Toni Morrison

Trent has been home for a month.

The first morning in our new home, he needed a toaster and we had none. Trent eats honey and peanut butter on toast every morning for breakfast, so he walked outside in his bare feet to the garage sale happening across the road, and he bought a toaster for two dollars, came home, and had breakfast.

It's taken us a month to get used to each other again. For me to get used to Trent's fidgeting and the way he leaves his clothes lying on the floor and for him to get used to me leaving paint on the kitchen table where I do my canvases.

Having an Alberta teacher's certificate, he's waiting to be approved by the Ontario Board so he can work, which means many empty days at home while I freelance on my laptop. It's crowded here, in our bungalow.

So come October, I fly to Sydney, Australia, to visit my sister Allison.

I fly because I've spent three months caring for Mum, and I'm so empty I've turned inside-out.

Allison meets me at the airport, and she looks beautiful, with her long wavy brown hair and wide blue eyes. She looks like Dad's mom, like Grandma Dow when she was young.

We take the train into the heart of Sydney. I am jet-lagged but tired of sitting so we wander the wharf, the cobblestone path, past tiny shops and down to the water where the glass Opera House lights up the sky and Aborigines, dark-skinned natives of Australia with painted warrior faces, sit telling stories through music. They tell "Dreamtime" stories, using voice, clapsticks, and the didgeridoo, and the air smells like sunscreen.

Allison takes me to a tea shop where we fill up our thermoses and then we visit the touristy places along the water. I consider buying some overpriced postcards and we take the bus back to her yellow townhouse in the suburbs, surrounded by manicured lawns and parks in Baulkham Hills, within walking distance to Hillsong International Leadership College where Allison is a student.

I go for a run that night along the paved path in the dark, straight into a cloud of bats. I scream and cover my head, run back to the house terrified, take a long shower. I sleep on the floor in Allison's room and we spend hours praying for Mum and catching up on life together, and after a few days of catching up and meeting her friends and surviving the blistering sun, because it is turning summer there, we rent a car.

We rent a small white Toyota, put a teddy bear on the dash for our mascot and we learn to drive on the opposite side of the road.

We get lost and I get irritated and Allison, in her patient way, puts up with me and we map out a trip.

Then we go home, grocery shop, pack our hiking bags, and take off for the coast, one and a half hours away, to Kiama. Once there, we camp. As we are setting up our tent, kangaroos bound through the site. "Oh, kangaroos," I say. Then I look again. "Oh! Kangaroos!"

We spend the next day walking the white sands of Kiama and swimming in the ocean. And we wander toward some rocks at the far end of the beach where we meet George, a tanned, naked old man with a towel around his middle.

He looks at my bare feet and says, "I can tell you have good character, because of the strength of your arch." And then he tells us this beach is his home. He comes here every day to read and to sit in the sun and he is as brown and wrinkled as the desert, his beard covering half his face and his pebble eyes lighting up when he laughs. He is retired, has been in the army and has seen the world, but he says there's nowhere more beautiful than this exact spot in Kiama.

We drive ten hours north, the next day, wearing long earrings and singing at the top of our lungs, the windows rolled down and us, passing long stretches of palm trees and brilliant red blossoms and kangaroo and koala crossings. Gas is "petrol," and instead of yield it's "give way," and instead of passing lanes they are "overtaking lanes."

Spring is in the mountains in the roar of red foliage and we stop to hike a forest and then find our way to a cozy mountain town, Mount Victoria, where we stay at an old-fashioned inn, The Imperial Hotel, with its ornate, overpriced rooms.

I miss Trent. For all of the beauty and the sightseeing I wonder why I've come, and I feel the Lord whisper, *To bring Allison home*, because I fear Mum is dying. And before I came Allison didn't know how bad Mum was because Dad didn't let on, over the phone. But I tell her everything and I beg her to come back for Christmas.

But it isn't just for Mum that I am here. It is for my sister, whom—for all of my years of anorexia and then recovery and dating boys and traveling afar—I've never really heard or seen. And this girl with the piano fingers who can play by ear, who is a musical gift, is lonely in Australia and needed family to make the trip to see her. To truly see her.

God's plan is never just about us.

Everyone we meet on our trip is friendly. They say "G'day" and "Mate" and "Massive."

And everywhere are fellow backpackers and strange-sounding birds.

We drive back to Sydney after a soft sleep at the hotel, where we trade in the car for a train pass. We spend a few nights back at Allison's house and then take the train down to Nowra, a small coastal community, where we stay with Allison's friend Shelly.

Shelly drives us to the white sands of Jervis Bay—a surfing, whale-watching paradise. Never was there more tranquil blue nor such stretches of sand. We lie and toast in the sun on Saturday and record a CD for Mum on Sunday, after church, our voices blending in soprano and alto.

Then we ride the bus back to Kiama, where we settle in a quiet little motel, purchase some groceries, and lay on our towels on the beach.

The sun brilliantly bright, the surf up, the rolling green hills sheltering us as humpback whales leap across oceans.

The following morning we take a taxi to 7 Mile Beach where we pay to learn how to surf in two hours. Our instructor is a short man from Bali who is patient and adept with the board. We slide into wet suits and, with a boy named Duncan watching the waves and telling us when to ride, we scale the surface of the water.

Allison and I are very similar. We both have hearts that long after beauty and we both desire serenity and the arts. Our voices sound good together, but because we're so similar we have to give each other space and a lot of time is spent silent on our towels, just watching the sun move across the sky or reading books bought at a local street vendor's table, and I worry about her eating habits while I'm there.

I worry, because I never used to. For all of my spending four years as a child starving myself, I didn't think about the way my sisters would be affected. In Sydney I realize Allison has become very careful about what she eats.

And I blame myself.

So some of the time is spent worrying and trying to get her to eat and yet most of it is spent laughing and telling stories and singing and praying.

I still remember holding her as a baby. The only one of us to be born with dark brown hair, her cheeks so rosy, and she'd trusted me when I'd held her. She'd looked at me with those deep blue eyes, those old-soul eyes that my son now has, and then I'd let her down.

I hadn't been an older sister to her. I've missed too many years, and am trying to make up for all of that.

She had my younger sister Meredith though.

Allison and Meredith shared a bedroom and they'd pretend to be horses, galloping from one bed to another and they both thought if they could jump high enough they'd be able to fly.

Sometimes, when we were being punished, Mum would tie us to the ends of our beds—just a long string attached to our leg and to the post—and whoever was tied up, the others would come and sit around and read stories to or play games with, in order to keep them company.

There were things like this, or Mum washing out our mouths with a bar of soap when we said words like "fart" or "friggen." And there was Dad using the belt on me when I refused to let his hand or the wooden spoon make me cry.

And he'd always close the door and spank us in his office, which didn't help with my relationship with the church either.

But there were good things too.

There was Dump Day. We'd drive with Dad in the minivan to the local heap of garbage and see if any treasures could be salvaged from people's wastefulness. This was how we found our first television set.

It went directly down to our basement, to be stored for movie night, which coincided with bath night. Saturday after supper we'd slip into the bathtub, scrub ourselves with Ivory soap, then pull on fresh pajamas stiff from the clothesline.

Mum would make bowlfuls of popcorn and we'd squish together, a clean line of sardines, and dip our hands into the bowls while the black and white television sputtered and slowly came to life. We'd rent a VCR and classics from the library, and Dad would constantly fiddle with the hookup throughout the movie, tinkering with the sound and the sharpness of the picture, while we kept our saucer-eyes glued to the screen.

Being pastor's kids, we lived in many houses. One had a fireplace. I can still hear the crackle of the logs, see the red-orange flames licking the wood, smell the smoky fire mingling with the baby-powder freshness of our skin as we huddled on the faded couch watching *The Wonderful World of Disney*. Those were days of innocence, laughter, and cozy happiness.

And there was Christmas morning with the stockings bulging and Dad reading the holy story and Mum's homemade cinnamon buns and the little cereal boxes we fought over because the rest of the year we were only allowed granola for breakfast.

There were picnics, and elaborate birthday cakes, and there was Mum reading us *Pilgrim's Progress* and Dad singing to us in his beautiful tenor and strumming his guitar.

And there were day-old donuts while driving home from church, even though Dad often had to pull over to spank one of us for being lippy in the backseat after a long Sunday morning.

Allison and Meredith were always quiet, because Keith and I were so loud, and Mum encouraged Allison to play piano when she wanted to play the violin. So even though she's so gifted now at the ivories, she longs for the strings, and she's never really been given a chance to talk at the dinner table.

So I'm trying.

I'm trying to hear her.

But I know those memories will always be there.

Those memories of me sitting and sketching inside, alone, at the cottage at Caufield Lake while Allison and Meredith and Keith played in the woods. Those memories of me slamming my bedroom door after fighting with Mum and Dad, while Allison and Meredith knelt in their bedroom praying that I wouldn't commit suicide, that I would someday let them hug me again.

"Thank you for letting me hug you, now," Allison says as we say goodbye at the airport the day I fly back to Canada. It's been three weeks and it's time. We've traveled north and south and surfed and hiked, watched whales and sung choruses in the chapel at Hillsong. We've scaled mountains and visited the local zoo where we saw koalas, panda bears, and wombats.

But it's time.

I tell her how proud I am of her. I tell her how beautiful she is. I tell her I'm sorry, for those years.

And she just shakes her head, says I have nothing to be sorry for, and she thanks me a thousand times for coming all this way. "You showed me how much I was loved," she said. "I needed that."

That's all we ever need, isn't it? To know how much we are loved. To know the lengths to which someone will go.

It just takes one person, believing in you. It just takes one person, loving on you. That's all it takes to change the world.

So I go home. To a man who let me come here in the first place. To a man who moved to a little town in Ontario so we could take care of my mum. To a man who's gone to all lengths to show me the span of his embrace.

I go home, to love.

30

Miracle

Canada: Blyth, Ontario

December 2007

> Eucharisteo—thanksgiving—always precedes the miracle.
>
> Ann Voskamp

It's Christmas and we're shopping, piling rolls of paper and chocolates and candy canes, stopping now to let Mum rest, and then on to the rows of Pillsbury dough and eggnog. I'm pulling Mum's hand away from the stacks of Toblerone and she's getting that look, the one that says we need to go home so she can sleep, but we haven't even started on main gifts, let alone dinner.

She laughs as we help her to the rusted van, Allison—who's flown home from Australia—and I. The snow is falling. Mum reaches out, shaky. The flakes melt fast on her skin, making her sparkle. Whenever I look at her hands, lined and worn, everything seems okay.

We sing carols in the car on the way home and Mum's cheeks are as red as Rudolph's nose, her eyes blue like a robin's egg, and Jesus is born in the seats and the song and the air between us.

Mum's got a glazed look now, and I know it will be hard to get her out of the car and into bed. We pull covers tight, pray angels be near and dreams be kind, and may she wake to attend the candlelight service—the same service we attended as children, dressed in outfits Mum sewed herself. I'll never forget my red velvet dress with the white lace collar, how fancy I felt in my eight-year-old skin. Dad would pull up the van, another rusted Chrysler, and we'd pile in and smile for thoughts of sugarplums and red plastic boots filled with candy come early morning; thoughts of pouncing on Mum and Dad, and then Dad turning the tree lights on; thoughts of stepping into the living room and wondering if angels had descended, for the glow.

The front door shuts, Dad shakes snow from the hat he's worn for twenty years and we watch him as he climbs the stairs, tired. He looks at us and we say, "She's down for a nap," and he swallows.

"How is she?"

"A bit fuzzy," I say, and he nods. Maybe we should decorate the tree.

But Allison insists on waiting for the others, for Meredith and Keith and his family to arrive. I call up Trenton and he brings the turkey. I baste it and stuff it for tomorrow's feast, for as much as Mum is fuzzy, it's Christmas, and I'm hoping for a miracle.

The gym is colored with candles and wreaths and a wooden nativity scene. Dad is preaching about the long-awaited Messiah and I'm propping up Mum, praying she wakes soon. The children act out the Christmas story and a family stands to light the Advent wreath, the final candle, and the mother in that family stands so tall and sure of herself. She needs no one to prop her up and they're all smiling, and I feel like crying. Where is Jesus in the dying? Where is his promised resurrection?

We're all together now, my brother and his wife and their children, my two sisters, and my husband. We make a long row of children praying into the silent night, holy night. And I remember years ago, Keith and I giggling, wondering what would happen if we touched candle flame to the hair of the lady in front of us; I remember Mum smiling and hushing quiet and looking up at Dad with tired eyes, her fingers sore from sewing.

Dad puts Mum to bed now, brother carrying her legs, husband helping to lift, and we all silently beg for her to be fine in the morning. But no one says anything. Instead we watch *A Charlie Brown Christmas*, and then we tuck into bed, too excited to sleep, for we all become kids again on Christmas Eve. We pretend to close our eyes as Dad puts red boots beside our pillows. I want to hug him and tell him he doesn't have to do this, he doesn't have to pretend everything is okay, but I don't because he's our dad. And Jesus is born in the placing of red boots stuffed with candy.

Morning, and we don't pounce on our parents' bed but trip upstairs to the hum of something holy. The lights are already lit, for we've risen too late, even though it's still dark outside. The air smells of coffee, and Mum and Dad are in the kitchen. Mum's eyes shine like tinsel as she touches my hair and says, "Good morning, beautiful," and everything in me sings hallelujah.

Stockings are first, and for me, they're everything, knowing Dad has wrapped each tiny gift—Mum thinking she has. We unwrap the deodorants and chocolates and toothbrushes we bought with her that day in the mall, and we exclaim because, at this age, the least becomes the greatest.

Dad pulls out his Bible and he reads the well-worn story. Mum fingers the nativity scene, the one that lights gold when the tea light flames. And we sing the morning bright, blending sopranos and altos and tenors. Mum's feet keep beat and Keith strums guitar, and we're a pajama-clad choir, baby Isaiah crawling underfoot on chubby legs.

We make cinnamon buns, iced sticky, gooey white, and we sit around the table and pull the flakey dough, savoring this being together. We've come from across the country, our usual reunions happening on computer screen, and this being able to touch each other's skin is something marvelous.

Mum is pouring us more orange juice and I think of how we used to only be allowed half a glass each, how I would long to drink as much as I could. But now, all I want is for her to be like this every day of the year. I'd drink as little or as much orange juice as she wanted, just as long as she felt better.

Then she looks at me with the same eyes she's always had and they tell me one day she will be better, and all because of a Baby born in a manger. And her eyes, they tell me she's still my mum, who says yes to me by smoothing my hair and calling me beautiful.

Later we serve turkey and stuffing and my head hurts from it all, and I wonder how Mum did it with four children in tow. I'm miffed when Granddad teases my lemon meringue pie, and I want to run away, but Mum touches my hand and I'm reminded of grace and I smile. Smooth my apron. Do the dishes.

We walk in the white of snow, our prints small in the soft of winter. Mum's dragging a little, but she's hooked arms with Dad and with me and we're singing again, "O Little Town of Bethlehem." We pass houses bright with lights, hills that sleds have slid, bushes frozen with December, and she's bundled tight in blue scarf . . . and I can't remember loving her more.

When we get back to the house, Mum unravels winter wear, serves us hot chocolate, and turns on some holiday classics. Soon, she's dancing. Dad swinging her this way, that, the string of Christmas cards rustling against their hair and the dusk falling slowly outside.

Tonight will be crackers and cheese and *It's a Wonderful Life*. Perhaps we'll play a game and then we'll tumble into bed, full, and tomorrow will begin the putting away and the packing up and the saying goodbye.

But right now, in this moment of dance and chocolate and Keith's small son eating paper; the lights blinking white, green, and red; and Frank Sinatra singing; in this moment, Jesus is born.

And I squeeze my husband's hand and sit as still as possible in a room full of motion. For this is my miracle. And I don't want to miss it. Not for the world.

Blyth, Ont.

July 23, 2003

Lord, please show me that my tumor isn't all for nothing; please use it to bless, to convict someone, and to bring you glory. Please make it clear soon. Otherwise it seems like such a selfish time for me and all work and trial for others.

31

Wanting a Baby

Canada: Ottawa, Ontario

March 2008

Nothing happens unless first a dream.

Carl Sandburg

I am a career woman now.

I am a staff journalist for the *Presbyterian Record* in Toronto and every month I drive two hours for a meeting and then two hours home. And one of my assignments is a story on *100 Huntley Street*, a talk show on Canada's Christian television network, and so I go to the station in Burlington, just outside Toronto, and interview the staff, and they learn of my story.

They learn how I starved myself as a child and as an adult, and how I found healing, and they put me on the show.

A couple of months later, in early May, I appear on *100 Huntley Street* and I talk about my story.

And Trent sits on a chair watching me, and following the interview, a pastor and his wife who'd been on before me and stayed to watch my segment ask if they can pray for us.

Because they'd heard me tell viewers that doctors said I probably wouldn't be able to have children.

The pastor is the son of a woman who had also been told she wouldn't be able to conceive, and so, in the back room of the studio, we all hold hands—the pastor, his wife, the host of the show, Trent, and I—and the pastor prays that we will conceive a son within the year.

I don't want children. I am a career woman and we have a nice life, Trent and I. But I nod and agree with the prayer and my eyebrows lift a little and then it is done. We hug, and we leave.

A few weeks later I am in Ottawa on assignment, covering a Presbyterian conference, when I receive a phone call from Trent.

Teneale, his sister, is pregnant.

Teneale, who wasn't supposed to be able to have children. She doesn't ovulate and yet here she is, pregnant.

I can't respond.

Sobs wring my body and I rock myself on the floor and I didn't know.

I didn't know I wanted a baby.

I didn't know I hadn't let myself admit it for the fear of not being able to have one.

After I hang up the phone I get so angry at myself, crying out to God in a tearful wreck of prayers, for how I've damaged my body. For how selfish I've been.

And the only thing that gets me through the night is a song by Imogen Heap, called "Speeding Cars." I put it on repeat.

> There, there, baby, it's just textbook stuff, it's in the ABCs of growing up.
> Now, now darling, oh don't lose your head, 'cause none of us were angels and you know I love you yeah.

The song is God, telling me he loves me. Telling me nothing can erase that love. That nothing I've done in the past can wreck my future so long as he is in it.

It seems too fast.

We buy a book on fertility and I purchase a thermometer, and after two months of trying we get pregnant at the end of August, on our family trip to Williamsburg, Virginia.

Upon arriving home, I realize I'm late, so I take the test four times, and four times, positive, the line faint but pink. And I can't help but feel suspicious because nothing good is ever easy.

But the joy outweighs the suspicion and we begin right away to pick out names and an African mobile and a bassinet in the secondhand store.

A wooden bassinette with white curtains and it looks like a fairy tale. The whole thing, a fairy tale, curling around my belly at night and talking to our son or daughter and reading Robert Munsch stories.

And at the end of every evening Trent places his hand where our Papoose lies and he prays a simple prayer.

"God, thank you so much for this new life. Take care of our child, we pray. Amen."

And I fall asleep dreaming of strollers and bikes and bottles. But try as I might, I can never see my baby's face.

We invite Dad and Mum one evening for pot roast and Grandpa Dow is there, too, alone—Grandma ill at home, in bed—and Trent tells them even as he says grace, "And we thank you, Lord, for the bun in Emily's oven," pausing as the words sink in and Mum hugs me so long that Trent begins to carve the meat.

Dad smiles and nods his head. "Congratulations, you two. May the Lord bless you," and then I turn to Grandpa—Dad's father—and his face is flushed, and he is crying.

"I never thought I'd see the day," he says. "You . . . you were so skinny, Emily, we didn't think you'd live to see your fourteenth birthday, and now this. It's a miracle."

I'd spent the summer of my thirteenth birthday at Grandma and Grandpa's. I became a skeleton while I was there, eating a peach for breakfast, a few pickles for lunch, and a scoop of corn for supper, skipping rope in the afternoons and going for long walks, and when I'd returned to Mum and Dad, at sixty pounds, they'd admitted me to the hospital.

Grandpa excuses himself, makes his way to the bathroom.

We look down at our plates and I subconsciously put my hand over my belly, trying to protect it all.

That Sunday we stand in church, share our news during praise and prayer time, and it is a small church, only thirty members, but they clap as though they are many.

I am eight weeks along, and I have a doctor's appointment in four more, and I wonder when I will begin to show. When will I need to buy maternity clothes, and aren't I supposed to feel nauseated by now? The suspicion throbs and I try to quiet my fears with prayer. Does God truly like to give us good things? Or is everything a test, a struggle, a suffering?

I begin a journal that night, a letter to my baby, and I scribble in blue ink my dreams for this child.

And I wake up crying, I wake up Trent, for I've dropped Papoose in my dream, and our child is gone. My womb, so very empty.

The blood appears, the next day.

It is the night of my first book launch at the local Christian bookstore and before leaving I go to the bathroom. Trent is playing squash in Goderich, thirty minutes away.

And the toilet paper is red when I pull it away.

I always liked the color red, until now. And I stand and look in the toilet and it's full of blood.

I practice saying to myself, "This must be normal," because my baby is still inside of me, I know this. Nothing has changed; there is just blood now. And blood is a sign of growth, isn't it?

But it is too bright.

I keep my legs closed as I walk to the phone, because I don't want any more of my insides falling out, and I call the health line. And they say to sit down and put my feet up and if I get cramps, to make a doctor's appointment.

They don't say the word. *Miscarriage.*

And I am grateful they don't because it would make it too real.

So I sit on the couch with my legs up and I call Allison, who is living at Mum and Dad's, and ask if she will take my place at the book launch, because I'm sick. She doesn't ask any questions, just says yes, and then I keep sitting still, and the cramps come.

My thighs and stomach cramp. I stare at the living room wall, at the wall I've painted crimson, the same color as the blood, and I'm thinking I should touch it up, that paint. But not now.

No, right now I have to sit very, very still or I might wake the baby.

And then, after two hours of sitting on the couch, I hear Trent pull up in our veggie car—a VW diesel that runs off of vegetable oil—and I hear the doorknob turn and him step onto the porch, pull off his runners, and then walk into the kitchen.

And suddenly he is standing in front of me. His hair is messed and his skin is flushed and he is looking at me. Then he kneels beside me, his forehead wrinkled.

"What's wrong?" he says. "I thought you were supposed to be at the bookstore. Are you okay?"

"Oh yes, I'm fine. I just can't move or I might drop Papoose."

And he begins to shake his head.

"There was blood," I say then.

I am so afraid he'll be disappointed with me.

"Oh, Em . . ." He puts his arms around me. "I'm so sorry."

"Be careful." I push his arms away. "You might hurt Papoose. It's just a little blood. This is normal. It has to be. It has to be."

Then my stomach seizes in another cramp and I know.

It's not normal. Papoose is not okay.

And I begin to shake.

Blue handwriting, scrawled across the calendar date: "13 weeks."

My mind drifts back to when I'd written those words, more than three months ago. I'd been painting a canvas for the baby's room—a picture still unfinished.

I had paused to scribble the reminder on the calendar.

But I need no reminder.

My baby would have been 13 weeks old today—officially past the "danger zone." *Would have been . . .*

I convince myself to sit down. Put my head in my hands and count to ten. "Not again," I whisper. I am so tired of crying. So tired of reliving the sadness. Yet it is only a Fisher-Price commercial away.

My baby is gone.

Trent tries to console me; he tells me the stats. He says that 15 to 20 percent of pregnancies end in miscarriage. This only makes me cry harder because it's all so impersonal.

Friends tell me their stories. I am shocked to learn one has gone through six miscarriages in five years. I take little comfort in the fact that mine is perhaps only the first of many.

Some say Papoose is waiting for us in heaven, alive and well. I just shake my head, turn away.

Heaven isn't enough right now.

They are just words—powerless words—unable to fight the grief.

An ultrasound confirms the miscarriage, confirms the bleeding of baby onto bed and nightgown and hardwood. Papoose died at five weeks. A woman in a lab coat scopes inside me, finding nothing but some dried up tissue and I think of the toilet paper, red on white, and has any of it been real?

Our prayers, crumpled with the paper in the garbage.

Wasted.

Trent has taken the day off school, and we leave the clinic to go to the beach.

We stop by my parents' house, down North Street, with the sign hanging from the tree that says "Quiet Waters," and Mum and Dad are both there when we walk in. Mum is having a good day.

I tell them what happened, and they don't understand. They've never miscarried, and Dad says, "Was there anything you could have done?"

And Mum hugs me then steps back awkwardly. "Was it because I hugged you too hard?" she says. "Is that why you lost your baby?"

We leave then, for Goderich.

We build an *inuksuk*, there, a stone memorial for Papoose. Pile rock upon rock for all of the dreams we had for her. Watch as waves hit the shore, lie on a blanket and cry for the baby that isn't. For the prayers over the womb. For the bassinet and the stories and the dreams.

And on the day when the placenta actually leaves my body, a burst of crimson and tissue, I read this verse in Psalm 113:9—"He settles the childless woman in her home as a happy mother of children. Praise the Lord."

The waves, crashing before me.

It is just a shoe, a pink baby shoe, but it breaks me like glass, weeks later, on the road on the way to Mum's, and I can't go on. I can only cradle myself against a tree as I would have cradled my child.

There is nothing truer than that child's life, nothing more real than my muscles making room for link of limb, and I feel deceived, a woman with a vacant womb and it is all I can do to pull myself home.

How full I'd felt, before, as though a baby had kicked and curled within. But it had only ever been a lie, a couple of ghost cells.

If I had known, I wouldn't have let Trent lay hands on my womb at night. I wouldn't have let him pray. And I wouldn't have claimed it to be a miracle after a lifetime of doctors saying I probably wouldn't conceive.

The doctors were right.

There was no miracle.

I have a dream that night.

I dream of a little girl, who's about a year old, sitting outside my bedroom door. She has yellow curls and she's playing with some blocks and when she looks up at me and smiles, she has Trent's hazel eyes.

And then I look down in my arms, and I see a baby. A baby boy with dark hair but I cannot see his face.

Trent holds my hand on the porch.

It is November and the grass and garden are covered in a dusting of snow and we are sitting in our brown chairs, close together, in the quiet of twilight. The air smelling like new things.

We have just found out that I have precancerous cells on my cervix, and I will need to get the cells removed the following week, and I wouldn't have been able to if I had still been pregnant.

I choose to see it as a silver lining. I choose to believe that maybe God is still with me. Maybe he still likes me enough to show me I *can* get pregnant—although I don't believe yet that I can stay pregnant—but knowing also that I needed those precancerous cells removed. Maybe he is turning the awfulness of miscarriage into the gift of saving me from cancer. Maybe.

Trent holds my hand and, after a little while, we go back inside and play checkers on the couch.

And in spite of everything my face is downcast and Trent, trying to reach me, somehow.

He leans close to me, says, "Hey, babes, good news . . ."

And I look at him, hopeful.

"What?"

"I love you," he says.

I smile.

Trent cups the moment, tender.

"Hey, babes, good news."

I wait.

"We own a beautiful little home."

I nod.

"Hey, babes, good news—we have a bed, and food, and families that love us."

I kiss his nose.

"Thank you," I say.

This is marriage; to be the stronger, when the other is weak.

And so, a beautiful tug and pull; a dance in the wilderness, two lovers leaning hard into each other in black air, leaning on all that is good and faithful, and seeking the light—the morning light—in each other's eyes.

32

Conception

USA: New York City;
Dominican Republic: Bonao

February 2009

You never understand life until it grows inside of you.

Sandra Chami Kassis

It happens in the Big Apple.

We've decided to do foster training, because I'm scared I can't keep a baby to full term and the pastor's prayer is just wishful thinking.

We learn of a local girl who is expecting a baby boy in May, and she is a drug addict who needs someone to adopt her baby.

So we meet with her. We sit with her on a picnic bench outside the respite home for pregnant teens, and we laugh with her. Tell her about us, show her our photo albums, then take her for ice cream at the local shop.

And she likes us, and we begin the procedure to adopt her son.

Meanwhile, we plan a trip to New York City for Valentine's Day, where we'll meet up with Stasha and Nicholas, who now live in Toronto.

We're driving our veggie car, which Trent converted after ordering a kit from the States, and the radiator steams on our drive to Toronto. We're leaking radiator fluid. We keep stopping to pour water in the radiator and then we hit bumper-to-bumper traffic, and we are fighting. Stressed. Our flight leaves at 2:00 p.m., and it is 1:00 p.m. by the time we reach the airport at a snail's pace and they won't let us through, and they put us on standby.

So we pray and wait for two seats to open up on the next flight and they do.

We fly into New York by 5:00 p.m. and take a taxi to our hotel and meet up with Stasha and Nicholas. We order Chinese, and then Stasha and Nicholas leave for the night and I turn to Trent and tell him I am ovulating if he wants to try and make a baby.

Because even though I'm scared, God is bigger.

Trent doesn't want to. He is still hurting from the fight, from hours earlier, but we make love in the hotel bed and then fall asleep.

The following days are spent on the streets of New York City, visiting the Wax Museum and the world's most famous burger joint and going to the Broadway show *Chicago*. We walk down Wall Street and see where the towers have fallen and I remember where I was, on September 11. In the sanctuary of The King's University College, in Edmonton, watching the news as a school, on a screen, and I was sobbing.

Not just because of the sorrow of lost lives but for the way the Spirit was grieving, for the way the Lord was longing for his people to turn to him.

So I stare at the ground where the towers had fallen, graders and trucks working the dirt, and signs proclaiming a resurrection of infrastructure, and I pray.

We find out a few weeks later.

The mother has changed her mind. She wants to try to raise the baby herself, and little do I know she'll lose him to the foster care system two months after giving birth on account of a party she holds in her apartment.

All I know is, my heart is cramping. It feels like another miscarriage.

And then I am late, and I take a test, and it is boldly positive.

We've conceived within the year, and we will find out later it is a boy. Just as the pastor prayed.

I am cautiously happy, but as the weeks come and go, and I turn nauseated from the hormones, I grow confident.

Then, more blood.

The dark kind.

I have a blood test taken, and it is the weekend so I have to wait for Monday. And I stay curled up on my bed, not moving, and Allison brings me Brennan Manning's book, *The Furious Longing of God*, and I read it in one sitting. It keeps me from losing faith.

And Monday morning at eight o'clock the doctor calls me and he tells me, good news, I am still pregnant—the dark blood was simply old blood from the implantation.

I know then that God is good in spite of evil, that we are going to be okay. That he does give good gifts, and he does turn ashes into beauty, mourning into comfort. He is the author of all things redeemed, and this child is a prayer that is being answered.

But the thing about God is, he sees the big picture. And that big picture is framed by grace and it includes us in it, and he cares more about refining our character and our spirits than he does about acknowledging our feelings. So sometimes he risks us not liking him for the sake of the bigger picture. For the better picture.

This past year God has been preparing us for a son who will be born November 12, 2009, a son whom the Spirit will declare to be a "tender-hearted leader."

We fly to the Dominican Republic during March Break to an adventure ranch called Rancho Wendy in Bonao. We arrive at midnight but can still see the tarantulas crawling across the cement floor of our room, and there are single bunk beds. Trent sleeps on the top and me on the bottom, and Trent's bunk bed breaks at three in the morning, waking me with a terrible soreness.

We end up laying our mattresses on the floor and praying the spiders won't find us.

Bonao is the gateway to Los Quemados, a cozy village in the foothills of the Cordillera Central, northwest of the national capital Santa Domingo. The men and boys sit outside their shacks talking in the bright heat, the women inside cooking or cleaning and kids and haunted dogs on the streets.

There are waterfalls and mountains and rope bridges and fruit plucked from trees and we jump from cliffs into rivers and hike across rocks and hot sand.

But then I burn my calf on the scooter we take up the side of a mountain and Trent gets bucked from the one horse at the ranch, and it rains. We are the only visitors there and the hosts don't speak English. We sit under the canopy playing cards at the picnic table and eating rice and beans for breakfast, lunch, and supper, and I cry. I'm so disappointed by the spiders and the burn and the bucking horse. And sometimes it takes disappointment to remember that this world is not our home.

I know God is here in the nature and the people, but more than that, he is within me. The kingdom of heaven is where I belong. It is where all of my journeys have been taking me. And no place on earth can match the welcome that is found in God's arms.

On the third day Trent rises and tells me he has a plan and we are leaving, he says, even though we've booked our room with the broken bed and the tarantulas for a week. We are leaving for the coast.

Trent's wallet gets stolen on the bus on our way to the coast, and I stand at the side of the road in Punta Cana with our bags while he chases down the bus on a scooter. Gets his wallet back from a passenger who won't look him in the eyes.

We both ride scooter taxis to the beach lined with resorts, and we find a bright place with yoga and organic meals and clean sheets just meters from the beach.

We discover a restaurant down the road run by an elderly couple that cooks us eggs every morning, just the way we like them, and we take our eggs to the beach and sit at a table and watch the water lap the shore.

I have morning sickness there on the coast and even as my stomach rolls with the waves and I lie flat on the sand I praise God for the way I can feel my baby growing inside me.

The world is a womb, a vacuous space, and there is life in the arms of tree stretching high touching sky, and everything pulses.

It's a boy.

I am eighteen weeks pregnant now, and at the hospital in Stratford for an ultrasound. I am so tired from sleepless nights, from aching joints, that I have nearly fallen asleep on the sheet as my son swims across the screen and I wake to the technician showing me the curve of stomach, my boy's long legs and lips pursing, chubby cheeks, and in spite of my fears—of not being able to show him enough love or to help him believe in God—I want this tiny boy with everything in me. Because he is: everything in me.

"Aiden," I say then, and this, the name Trent and I have chosen. "Aiden Grey." The name means "pleasant little fire," and I drive home through the womb that is earth and blare the CD loud, and the sky splits blue as though the eye of heaven is opening.

I lie in bed alone that night—Trent at a football game—and imagine our son.

I imagine he has brown hair, and he skips stones and is good to people—but *what if?* And I instinctively wrap my arms around him, trying to protect my boy from the world, from the school shootings and the drugs and the hatred.

All I can do is lie there and cry and pray that Aiden will have wider eyes than me, eyes wide enough to see all of life, to let in all of the light and the miracles, not just the pain.

It is the kind of love that holds the universe and it feels much like a fish only I know it has a heart and a brain and fingernails and it hiccups beneath the cover of my skin, and it is one of the greatest love affairs, this love between mother and child.

"I'm glad you weren't alone," Trent says when he arrives home to find me still awake, curled around our unborn.

A mother is never truly alone.

And this child is reminding me of the Holy Spirit that expands within, that grows with every cramp and swelling and ache, and even as I am physically filled with my son, I am spiritually filled with an eternal kind of life that I give birth to every day, in the way I live, in the way I speak, in the way I love.

The God of Abraham, Isaac, and Jacob knows us before we are. Before knitting us in our mother's womb, and it's this knowing that keeps us from getting lost.

It's this being known that is the compass that guides us home.

33

Better Is One Day

Canada: Blyth, Ontario

May 2009

> We might be wise to follow the insight of the enraptured heart rather than the more cautious reasoning of the theological mind.
>
> A. W. Tozer

I think it's possible to experience heaven on earth.

I believe God intended heaven to be a current possibility rather than a futuristic concept. I believe in eternal life, starting now.

These past twenty-eight years I've been in constant motion, ever doing, never resting, all for fear of wasting time.

I've often felt very distant from God. Detached. Like he doesn't hear, doesn't see, doesn't listen.

This morning I read Psalm 22:2, "My God, I cry out by day, but you do not answer." I thought to myself, *Exactly*.

Then I went for a run. A membrane of thin cloud stretched across the sky. Underneath my feet, gravel; at my sides, stretches of wheat fields as far as the eye could see. In my ears, the Swedish metal band Nightwish. Then all of a sudden, a thought that I could only attribute to God: *Remember when I said "Watch me take care of you"?*

And I did. I remembered. It happened while I was weeding Mum's flowerbed.

Trent is always telling me to live in the moment. I realized in that particular moment on that gravel trail that God was saying I had chosen not to hear him. I had chosen not to listen.

So I came home and decided to take a vacation from my worries. I was going to watch as God took care of me. I would live in the moment, thinking only about current events and choosing to enjoy myself, to rise above my circumstances and simply "be."

Why, I wonder, does God make us capable of fear and worry? Why does he let us go through such pain?

And then it comes to me. It takes going through hell to appreciate heaven. And on earth we have a choice. We can experience heaven on a daily basis; we can surrender our worries and let our minds and souls be flooded with peace, knowing someone divine is taking care of us.

Or we can hold on to control, for fear of letting go and letting God.

It's not about dying and someday going to heaven, it's about inviting heaven into our everyday existence.

Forgiving. Redeeming what is lost. Trusting. Letting go. Living now.

It's dark. I knock several times and no one answers.

I push open the door.

"Dad? Mum?"

Dad's grey head appears at the foot of the stairs. His eyes are pools. Why didn't he call? Why didn't he let me know that he needed me today? I should have known.

I step quickly inside and blabber, "What's wrong? Is everything okay?"

Dad shakes his head. "Fuzzy day."

He slowly climbs the stairs. Gives me a hug so huge I gasp, and when he lets go, his face is lined and old.

"Can I go see her?"

"Of course."

Her room is heavy with sleep, Dad's makeshift curtain across the window. I hear her first, snores so deep they make me shiver. Her face is pale, the sheet tucked up to her mouth, cheeks pasty, hair matted to her forehead, wet from sweat.

I whisper Mum's favorite prayer to myself: "God, grant me the serenity to accept the things I cannot change, courage to change the things I can, and wisdom to know the difference." Sit on the side of her bed, take her cool limp hand in mine and hold it. Keep whispering serenity over and over for fear I'll give up on God altogether.

How long will she be sick? How long, Lord? What will happen to Dad if she goes? Who will keep him from staying up too late on the computer? Who will make sure he eats healthy? That he eats at all?

Dad doesn't know how to say no, doesn't know how to quit, to slow down, to rest. He's a willing victim of the North American society we breed daily within ourselves. We want it but we pretend to resist it. We want it because it makes us feel like we matter. Plus we're scared of silence, of rest. Best to keep busy. And so we hate ourselves into an early grave.

I am guilty of it too, but since moving to Blyth and visiting with Mum, I've learned a new way of living. A way of being that requires simply breathing. I don't feel pressured to do anything right now except sit at Mum's side and watch her chest rise and fall and whisper a prayer for us all.

Soon I begin to hum—a hymn falling from my lips, as much as I don't want it to, and then the words leak out much to my dismay:

"Better is one day in your courts, better is one day in your house, better is one day in your courts than thousands elsewhere . . ."

How can I be singing this at a time like now? How can I be staring into the face of a dying woman victimized by her mother's own suicide and still believe in a gracious God? How can I profess . . . and then I'm down on my knees, crumpled on the floor unable not to worship, unable not to kneel at the feet of my Savior and my fists begin to pound the carpet while tears wail down my face.

After a while, I am spent. I pick myself up off the floor and wipe my face. Then I hear it. A soft moan from the bed. I quickly go to Mum's side; her eyes are still shut but her mouth is open. I lean closer. "Mum, are you okay?"

The faintest of smiles on her lips and with all the effort she can muster her hand lifts and strokes my cheek. "Better is one day . . ." The words are undeniably clear.

I begin to sob. Her hand stays on my cheek. I sit there, take her hand in mine, and begin to sing again. This time Mum's eyelids lift, revealing milky blue. And she sings with me. I see the blanket move and look down at her feet; they're poking out from under the covers, moving in time with the song.

I don't have the answers. I don't know how this story will end. All I know is that there is a very real God whom my mother adores, and if she, in all her pain and suffering, can still radiate worship, how much more should I? He sees the little sparrow fall. He sees my mum dancing to the rhythms of his grace, and he sees me in all my anger trying to love him in spite of it all. So I will continue to trust, even if it means letting her go.

The pink evening sun slips over Mum's shoulders like a lace shawl. She sits huddled inside her apron, carefully peeling an apple. Pauses to stop and listen to the conversation.

Her eyes are wide, like a newborn's. I gently remind her to peel, and she smiles. Shoulders shrugging. Returns to her apple for a few more seconds.

It's a pie-making bee. The ladies from the church are gathered in my mother's living room. Dad's spread a tarp on the floor, and we're slicing, dicing, and rolling.

Mum is flushed; I worry she's tiring. Again, like a child, she can quickly become overstimulated. Fuzzy.

"Do you need a glass of water?" I say, rising. She nods. I bring it to her lips and she drinks. Looks up at me gratefully. Tears spring.

How do I explain the pain in my chest every time I hug the woman who gave me life?

The way I wish I could excavate the tumor and fill her head whole again?

How do I explain the nights filled with tears on her fuzzy days, the way my faith has curled at the corners, tattered and old?

But it's more than that.

It's watching her sway in her favorite sweatshirt and her droopy trousers, baggy and blue.

It's wanting to stand in her slippers and feel the way she does—utterly content just to dance.

People say I'm good to her. But as a woman who's expecting her first child in November, I imagine it's much like it will be with my newborn. It's an honor—not a chore—to serve someone who reflects the very face of God.

St. Joseph Island, Ont.
July 11, 1988

We are camping in our tent trailer at Camp McDougall and it's a lovely setting for restarting my project of journal keeping.

It's supposed to be a way of getting to know myself better—something I really need to do even at thirty-two years old. I'm still not sure of so many things in my life. It's also supposed to help me mature spiritually; I pray God will help me in this. After reading John Michael Talbot's biography **Troubadour of the Great King** I realize I'm not progressing very well on my spiritual journey. Talbot likens a Christian's life to a gradual process requiring time and maturation, the climax coming when we meet Jesus. This is encouraging because I certainly don't feel like I've "got it made."

I'm impressed by the Franciscan way of life, ever since learning about St. Francis of Assisi when confirmed twelve years ago. I've admired his mission and simple way of life. As Talbot describes some of their ministry, it's a simple, caring "presence" that speaks to people, a quietness and gentleness of spirit, which I envy, that can love everyone and unselfishly minister to anyone in need.

Another book recently read, Charles Swindoll's **Improving Your Serve—The Art of Unselfish Living**, needs to be read and digested again. It's not a new concept; it's as old as Christianity, but it goes so much against the grain of our materialistic, me-first society.

It's wonderfully strange how so many books I've read lately tie in together, seeming to emphasize my area of concern for particular interests. **Living More with Less** has excellent examples of how to live more simply, ecologically and generously, freeing us from materialism, worry over belongings, fear of robbery, and especially freeing us to a quieter pace of life which makes possible more meaningful relationships with family and those in need.

34

Writer's Workshop

Italy: Lake Como

June 2009

There is no greater agony than bearing an untold story inside you.

Maya Angelou

I find out I've won, but I don't plan to go.

I've submitted a paragraph from my book to an online contest put on by author Elle Newmark; the prize is a trip to Como, Italy, for a fiction workshop with authors including my favorite, Janet Fitch of *White Oleander*.

I never win anything but this time I did. My piece of prose is good for a pat on the back but I can't justify the ticket—because airfare isn't included.

But then Dad finds out about the contest and says he'll help, because he wants me to go.

And Trent agrees it's a once in a lifetime trip. So I go, five months pregnant, and I'm still fighting morning sickness on the plane trip to Milan. My maternity shirt stretched across my middle. It's my first trip with my son, and my ankles swell from the altitude and I purchase compression socks at one of the airport stands.

I sit next to an Italian girl who tells me about her boyfriend, a man she's planning on breaking up with upon her return. I tell her about Trent and our two-year breakup and when we exit the plane she asks to take pictures with me.

I take a taxi then, to downtown Milan, and it's early evening. The streets are lined with window boxes full of flowers, people riding bikes, quaint coffee shops, old stone cathedrals, and shopping centers.

We stop in front of the inn and I climb the stairs, my ankles puffy, and I can't wait to lie down. My roommate opens the door. Her name is Darlene and she's single and middle-aged. A violin case sits in the corner of the room and she's short and slim with close-cut hair and glasses, and she smiles when she sees my belly. Welcomes me in and tells me she was just leaving for a walk, and to lie down and rest. We'll meet up for breakfast, if I fall asleep.

I do, and so we rise on the day we're meant to ferry out to the island, and my ankles are still puffy. We drink Americano coffee at a café down the street, eat some scones, talk about writing. We're both journalists. Then we walk to a local cathedral, marvel at the light catching stained glass, at the heavy silence within the walls. Darlene is Catholic, and her reverence is evident in the way she brushes the spines of the holy books and sits quietly in the pew.

Finally, we catch a taxi to the railway station, Milano Centrale, and from there, take the high-speed train to Como.

In Como we meet up with a number of other writers down by the wharf where we're purchasing tickets for the ferry that will take us across the water to the island of Lake Como, known for being home to George Clooney's cottage. The air smells fresh here, like fish and salt, not like the exhaust of Milan, and we find a table under an umbrella at a restaurant across the street. Order gelato and wait for the ferry while getting to know each other.

I'm the only Canadian.

There's one Australian, and twelve Americans.

I decide that I don't like gelato. But it's cold and refreshing, and my ankles are still puffy and I miss home in spite of the sun glinting off the water.

The ferry takes us across the blue to an island full of wharves and boats and climbing streets and waterfront restaurants. Our hotel is just a short walk from the ferry and Darlene and I find our room, a large, spacious place with two queen-sized beds and a balcony overlooking palm trees and the lake. On the front lawn are row upon row of beach chairs, full of ladies in hats sunbathing, and waiters carrying trays of espresso and wine.

Darlene is pulling out her violin. She's going to play by the water. We have all evening to do what we want; the next morning we'll meet at a villa to begin the workshop.

I go for a walk on the boardwalk, past the boats. An older man is fishing with his son at the end of a wharf. Leaning on the rails are two men: a tall man in red pants, and a short stocky man in blue. Their shirts are tucked in, and they're studying the sky. I try to step quietly past but they turn, watch me go. Beside me, cars ramble past on a cobblestone road, and there's a statue of Mary surrounded by candles and flowers.

Down the boardwalk, farther, there's a pizza shop with tables outside and in, and the smell of crust and cheese and sauce. My stomach rumbles and I continue, down and around the lake, and it will be a walk I take daily, this path by the water. Bright yellow flowers cluster along the edge of the hill to my right, and then, a stone tunnel full of beautiful graffiti. I emerge on the other side and make my way past a couple of lovers leaning against the rails and my hand finds its way to my womb.

At the end of the path, another restaurant, this one more rowdy with lamps hanging over each table and wine bottles and laughter. I turn before anyone can see me and find my way back to the hotel.

That night I'm so tired I just stay in the room while the other writers do supper together. I'll always regret this. This sitting on my bed, writing, the sound of glasses clinking through my open window and the sea washing against the shore, but at the time, it was what I wanted.

Sometimes, though, what we want isn't best for us.

It would have been best for me to have joined the group as they did a twelve-course authentic Italian meal complete with appetizer and dessert.

Instead, I eat trail mix.

Come morning my ankles are less swollen.

I rise with the sun, draw the white blinds, and Darlene is already up and dressed, grabbing her laptop, and I pull on a summer dress.

Read my Bible on the balcony.

Downstairs we pile our plates with eggs and yogurt and fruit and then step onto the veranda that circles the hotel. We order Americanos from the waiter, and it isn't long before other writers join us and we are a loud laughing mess of tourists and the coffee is thick and dark and the sun is warm.

And across the lake, the mountains tear jagged into cloud.

We brush our teeth in our rooms then meet together, again, a few men among the group, to find our way to the villa—Casa Lenora—rented by the host of the workshop, author Elle Newmark of *The Book of Unholy Mischief*.

The streets are unmarked and skinny, and tiny Italian cars swerve past at seventy miles per hour. We walk in single file and houses line the road, villas with flowers and vegetable gardens. Old women with wrinkles and aprons wave hello; men sit smoking pipes and nodding. And then, across the street, Elle's gated home. A cream colored two-hundred-year-old structure with tall, shuttered windows that stretch up to the ceiling and overlook baskets of gangly blooms.

Inside, there's an airy sunroom encircled by chairs and then a hallway to a large kitchen with a stone floor and massive hearth, a large wooden table with a basket full of crusty bread and cheese and fruit and vegetables. And everywhere, there is light.

Men and women are sitting and drinking espresso, and making notes in the margins of manuscripts. And French doors, leading out to a patio surrounded by flowers and bushes.

It's any writer's dream.

Elle is short with olive skin and bright eyes and she claps her hands and calls in a singsong voice for us to join her in the front room. We sit around the circle on couches and chairs, and she welcomes us to Lake Como, and we study the faces of those we're being taught by.

There is bestselling author Janet Fitch, who is warm and quiet and wise, and Drusilla Campbell, a tall, elegant women's fiction writer, as well as Mark Clement, a horror writer with a booming voice who bursts into "When the moon hits your eye like a big pizza pie," and engages in deep heartfelt conversation. He tells us it's not about writing what comes naturally to you. It's about exploring what scares you. And I think about the night before, about my dinner of trail mix. About the fears that bind me.

The first night of the workshop, Elle hosts us for dinner down at the waterfront at a long table where we have a choice between fresh fish and pasta, and water or wine made from local grapes. For dessert, tiramisu.

The teachers are so real I can smell their perfume, and across the table sits Janet, the author of my favorite book, with a swooping black hat, winding her pasta around her fork and talking about her daughter back in California.

Halfway through the meal I end up leaning across my *spaghetti alla carbonera* (spaghetti with bacon and eggs) and telling her about my mum. She asks me questions and listens. Like a friend.

Over the next few days, she'll teach us how to describe things using all five senses. We go on assignment, writing about our local surroundings and then gather together and read out loud what we've written. Mine is almost always poetic, and we are all writers, and we're all learners, and the authors are honest about how hard it all is.

Elle's book was originally self-published and then, when she did the launch on Amazon and blew sales out of the water, major publishers got into a bidding war over her novel.

It took Janet Fitch ten years to publish a short story. Now she has a book recommended by Oprah.

Another night, we're dining over a five-course meal and she pauses. Asks us, "Who do you suppose they are?" She's talking about the couple at the next table. So we imagine who they are, bringing characters to life.

Our work is critiqued and shared that week. We eat personal pizzas and pasta and fresh cheese on buns. We laugh and cry and go for hikes and purchase silks downtown on our afternoon off, taking the boat to the shopping district. I buy Aiden an expensive pair of blue knitted booties, and a cashmere shawl for myself, as well as a small bottle of wine to open when our son is born.

The final dinner is somber and long. The owner of the restaurant begs Elle to leave: "Signora, I have to go to bed," and we pile out, taking photos with the authors whom we call by first name, and saying our goodbyes.

I'm anxious to get home.

My boy kicking against the inside of my ribs and my body lonely for Trent's.

But I want to stay here too, within the fortress of mountain and tree and yellow flower. The cobblestone streets and fishermen, and the quiet camaraderie of writers.

"One day," I whisper to Aiden as we take the high-speed train back to Milan, back to the airport, back to Canada. "One day, we'll return to Italy. The world, my son, is our oyster."

I am learning though, that it is more than that. It is so much more than having resources or oysters or passports. No matter how many flights I take, no matter how many countries I visit, if God's will and heart are not my ultimate destination than I am to be more pitied than anyone.

35

Giving Birth

Canada: Stratford, Ontario

November, 2009

> So how on earth can I bring a child into the world, knowing that such sorrow lies ahead, that it is such a large part of what it means to be human? I'm not sure. That's my answer: I'm not sure.
>
> Anne Lamott

It's been nine months and my stomach is distended and veined, and the days are long.

"It's time!" Trent slides across the kitchen floor in knitted slippers, grabs some lime nachos, homemade zucchini salsa, and a bottle of home-brewed beer; runs back to the living room.

It's time for our evening show together. We sit close, feet touching, watching a sitcom, laughing, his hand on my womb.

But my mind is far away, wondering when, and how; worrying about labor pains and latching.

Then it's to bed, and rising; another day. Another day of waiting.

I stop. Pray: "Lord, fill up my day. Not my will, but yours."

Suddenly, a phone call. Mum is on the other line, asking me to come for tea, not five minutes after my uttered prayer. "Of course," I say. She is delighted.

We sit—her in the blue padded chair, me on the couch. I look at Mum, and she smiles. We drink Earl Grey and discuss books; she is surrounded by piles of them. *Anna Karenina* is her favorite. And when it's time to go, I confess, "Mum, I asked God what he wanted me to do today. And then you called. I think he wanted me to spend time with you."

She's standing now, shaky. She laughs. Holds out her arms. "Of course. He wanted you to give me a hug."

So simple. This, Lord? Is this what you want from us? Even as we wait, to serve; to embrace moments such as these. Moments spent drinking tea. Moments spent hugging. Moments spent touching feet and laughing.

This, then . . . this loving while waiting. This is joy.

"Can I hold the baby?" Trenton says.

I smile, wishing he could, yet somehow wanting to cling to my tiny companion who swims and sings within me, whose foot is pressed against my side long after the world has fallen asleep.

And part of me cries at the thought of labor, the thought of losing this speechless connection with the life within.

I rest, hand on abdomen, feel him kiss my palm. I poke him when he's too quiet, and he reassures me with a gentle kick, and as water drips from showerhead onto belly I watch my skin ripple with infant motion.

I am starting to understand the concept of second birth—the one God desires of us.

To be born again; to become like infants in God's womb, entirely dependent, utterly quiet, never alone. Wordless communication, unspeakable love, cushioned against the world's blows.

Grace within the belly of our Maker.

They say that becoming a parent means watching your heart walk around outside of your body.

On November 12, I finally gave birth to my heart.

In that moment, that searing second where Aiden's head appeared and my lungs collapsed, it was as though I finally understood: love with skin on.

I am a broken woman. I humbly, with utmost adoration, crawl up to the cradle of my son and peer over, seeing only this holiness of heaven, and wondering how I, a mere mortal, might bear the wisdom necessary to raise this fragile person.

I cry when he hiccups. I fear for his life while pushing his stroller down the sidewalk. I lie awake at night listening to his breathing, worrying he has a cold.

It has been three days.

The next eighteen years are going to be long. Each day, I will be forced to give up my heart, trusting God to watch over the boy he's entrusted to us.

The delivery process was one of delirium and pain, blood and tears.

The world was white with snow the day Aiden's head tore through, thirty-six hours after being induced and then, having my water broken because my body's stubborn that way, and finally, the epidural.

It began Monday, November 9. I had asked God to prepare me for the day when I would give birth. Every morning Trent and I read one chapter of the Bible together. This particular morning it was John 16:21. "A woman giving birth to a child has pain because her time has come; but when her baby is born she forgets the anguish because of her joy that a child is born into the world."

Later that day when I visited the doctor in Stratford, she asked me if I'd like to be induced. Previously breech, Aiden had decided suddenly to turn, head-down. The doctor thought we should seize the moment. I agreed—but could I go home and grab my bags?

The following day I was given Cervidil, twice, softening the cervix, then returning home to sleep.

Wednesday morning we woke early and drove back to the general hospital with the car seat in the back.

"This time you won't be leaving without a baby," the nurses told me.

The doctor broke my water.

I was put on an IV: synthetic oxytocin, dripping into veins, forcing harsh contractions. I bore it, gritting teeth, through the Comedy Network and playing a game of Agricola with Trent and the nurses, until 8:30 at night when I was too tired to stand and rock, too tired to breathe out the pain, and so—the epidural.

With that, chills. But peace. And deep, crazed sleep.

I had been contracting since 8:00 a.m. and it was now 10:30 p.m. and I'd only dilated two centimeters, putting me at three cm total. I needed to be at ten to birth my baby. The doctor stood tall above me, kindly face, suggesting a C-section.

"Sounds good," I said, groggily. I didn't want a C-section but I didn't have strength to argue.

"How about waiting half an hour?" Trent said.

And so we did, and I vomited four times, followed by more chills and then the nurse's face over mine telling me the vomiting had forced Aiden's head to shift and press against the cervix. I'd dilated three more centimeters in forty minutes. Another twenty minutes, and I was at 9.5, and then, they told me to push.

And I did. Red-faced hard. Sweating. Twenty-four minutes of thinking every breath would be my last, of feeling like dying, of knowing that something huge depended on me doing this but wondering, did I really care anymore?

Then, his head. His beautiful head of brown hair. Slimy body on mine, curling up in a frigid fetal position and the first frozen cry. I did care. And there was nothing I cared about more.

I gave birth to love. And now, I get to watch it grow. Every day, for the rest of my life.

I had wanted the moment to be magical but it was mostly messy and yet, when they laid him in my arms and he looked up at me with his father's eyes, it was everything.

The time was 12:01 a.m., November 12, two days overdue and the world was white and my bedsheets red, but I held a baby in my arms, all eight pounds, two ounces and twenty inches of a child the doctors didn't believe I could have, and he latched right away.

And I heard God whisper out of the darkness, *See how much I love you.*

Even as flesh ripped and life gave way to life and crying and pushing and breathing and Trent gripping my hand, asking if there was anything he could do.

God loved me, and this love sustained through the night and morning when fetal heartbeat turned infant skin and the belief that life was over became final push and I knew—it was all only beginning.

And when it was over and I heard the gasp and curdling cry, my body rested, like God on the seventh day, knowing it was good.

God sang over us, sang his love over us even as we drove home to the bassinet and the African mobile, to begin life as shell-shocked parents. Sleep-deprived and scared.

And I knew what it was for love to be stretchy. To wrap long and wide, around. My nipples were sore and cracked, but I tucked Aiden close and fed him and we'd sleep, curled up against each other.

We spent the first two days in the hospital just staring at each other, the nurses teaching me how to nurse and Mum and Dad coming to visit, and the nurses taking Aiden away at night when he wouldn't sleep, so I could.

I wanted to take those nurses home with me.

And Grandpa and Grandma came to visit the second day, and they cried over Aiden and beamed and said he was beautiful.

And I thought of Nanny, and how she'd missed the art that was her children, right in front of her, for all of her wanting to be an artist.

How she'd missed the beauty in the lines of her children's jaws, in the swinging of their arms, in the graceful dance of their limbs.

And I picked up Aiden, almost reverently, said into his wide unblinking eyes, "You are my greatest creation."

I break while Aiden sleeps, partly due to the hormones and my stomach not shrinking, and partly for remembering what I've put my own mum and dad through; my dad, who's holding Aiden and looking at me and saying, "I'm so proud of you."

Mum, who keeps smiling and kissing my cheeks and telling me how beautiful I am, how beautiful Aiden is.

And I beg forgiveness from them both, forgiveness for those nights when I was nine, ten, eleven, twelve, and starving for all of the pain of feeling unloved. Their baby girl, yelling and slamming doors and refusing to eat, and what do you do when your child won't eat? When the life you gave birth to, when the baby you grew wants to die?

And I fear my son getting my genes and I can't stop hugging him, my Aiden Grey. I can't let him go.

Trent feels the same kind of love, only with less fear.

A couple of years later, when I am expecting our second son, Kasher Jude, Trent writes this letter to Aiden in his baby book:

> I will always love you and I am so proud of you. I pray that we will always have fun together like we do right now. I hope you will be able to trust me with your hopes, dreams, fears, doubts, and worries. You are an amazing child of God. I am so excited to be able

to watch you grow up and to see the man you will become. I love you. Daddy.

Nights later, in the nursery, I rock, the world a spindle of mothers, unraveling in house coats and tousled hair, bodies nursing babies and the thread of life on a milky cloth.

I think of my mum and how she'd given herself for me, how she'd given body and midnight to me and how I had clung, as Aiden does now, and how Mum had prayed.

I know she prayed, for Dad has shown me Mum's journals, diaries she'd kept as her children aged. The journals scrawled in prayer in faint blue by hands that were never still. Such kind hands, and they would fold over my infant body as I nursed.

And those journals speak of those nights, of those prayers, of her body swaying to keep herself awake and her mouth mumbling things of the soul, this young believer who'd become a Christian just a few years earlier, and it is all I really know too, this mumbling.

For what else can a mother do in the face of the night?

And God is in these small graces, I think. In the infant slurps and the whispered prayers, in the hands cupping cheeks and the rocking of chair, in the blanket swaddling, diaper changing, bath drawing, fever-soothing touch, he is: for God is all anyone ever has.

Trent serves me in the coming days and months, as does his mother Marge, who flies to Ontario for three weeks and sleeps in our heated front porch on a bed we borrow from my parents because we have no guest room.

And one day when I am crying because I feel overwhelmed, Aiden in my arms, Marge takes my face in her hands and covers my cheeks with kisses and promises me everything is going to be okay.

And I believe her.

Trent comes from a family that loves extravagantly.

And I am learning to receive that kind of loving.

But still, Marge has to keep trying to convince me to eat because I've cut back to cans of creamed corn or one slice of toast because I want my stomach to disappear and my old jeans to fit.

I lose the weight too quickly and find it hard to sleep again. And one day, when I'm looking in the fridge and see half a muffin, and remember how for lunch I'd only allowed myself the other half, with a couple slices of cheese, I realize I am sliding backward. And I have a son now. A son who sees me. Who sits in his bouncy blue chair and blows bubbles at me and watches me restrict.

So I begin to listen to my body again. The way I did when I was pregnant, when my body would sob for protein or calcium or fruit. Its voice isn't as loud anymore, but it's still there.

And Trent keeps serving me, doing dishes and making meals, and it is his way of saying, *I wish I could do more. I wish I could have lain on that bed and given birth to our child so you didn't have to. I'm sorry you had to go through such pain.*

I had wanted him to carry the pain for me, and he wasn't able to. And I'd held it against him, secretly, until realizing he would have done it for me in a heartbeat.

And this too is part of the curse, that man, made to protect and defend his wife and family, cannot carry female agony. Cannot always protect his wife, can sometimes only watch.

36

Healing

Canada: Blyth, Ontario

March 2010

> Live, then, and be happy, beloved children of my heart, and never forget, that until the day God will deign to reveal the future to man, all human wisdom is contained in these two words, "Wait and Hope."
>
> Alexandre Dumas

Doctors are saying the tumor has nearly disappeared, and everyone is calling it a miracle but Mum doesn't feel miraculous. She still can't cook supper and she still thinks it is Sunday.

Mum knows I have a boy now but she can't remember his name and he seems to know her, gripping her finger when we put him in her lap, her arms too weak to hold him long and he smells like fabric softener.

She wishes she could buy her grandbabies nice things and make me casseroles and remember how old the baby is but she doesn't want to ask in case I think she doesn't care enough to remember, and she does, she really does.

Today Mum dresses herself. It takes an hour, but she has on her stretchy pants and her shirt is clean and she's even brushed her teeth and it is tea time.

Mum's made me a mug too, because I am coming over to visit, and maybe we'll watch a movie. She wants to hold me like she did when I was young, folded to her heart, because it is all happening so fast, this life.

Mum is sitting, now, and picking up a Karen Kingsbury book and waiting for me to arrive, and she should find her glasses for the movie and maybe afterward we will go to church.

It gets so lonely some days but that is okay because she has Dad, and she knows people find it hard to sit with her because she forgets the words and she sometimes falls asleep while they are talking.

And she should water the plants.

Someone is at the door, and Dad is there already, answering. Mum recognizes my voice, and she tries to get up from her chair but suddenly her legs won't move and all she can hear is the music. She was so good just a minute ago and she wants to give me my tea but she is just too tired.

They say she is a miracle, that the tumor is gone, but Mum doesn't see it.

Mum wore skirts and patent leather shoes and sat shy in front, in calculus class at Guelph University. And she blushed pink and Dad needed to know her, this woman with the accent, and so he did.

He knew her slowly, biking miles on country roads to bring her flowers and God in a soil-thumbed Bible and kissing sweet under Ontario's sky.

And now he bows low to massage her feet as she hums off-key, and they watch British comedy while she touches his hand beneath the afghan.

Mum, who schooled her children at the kitchen table, who hung laundry every day and served as church secretary, Sunday school teacher, church librarian, and pastor's wife. Mum, who sometimes forgot what day it was, or how to walk.

But the tumor is shrinking, after eight years of growing, and she is rising again, out of bed and into a new dawn, and she is learning how to walk, how to bake, how to clean, again, and she is hanging laundry on the line and dressing herself and telling Dad she loves him.

Mum and babe, asleep.

Mum wrapped under feather-down in my bedroom; babe in bassinet, under a blanket of soft blue.

Mum is here, for Dad has gone to work. She stares up at me from her pillow, eyes bright, loving me.

On good days, she holds him: my Aiden. He feels the heart of his grandmother beating through her favorite navy sweater. She curls her finger around his. He knows nothing of her tumor and everything of her love.

And for now, they sleep. Left in the hush of the afternoon, I warm up some soup and eat it, looking out the window at winter rain, breathing deep the circle of life.

I was told recently about a child who lives in Alberta and claims to see angels. This boy is not prone to the fanciful. He is alert, rational, and serious. But he sees angels. One day, he turned on the music in the living room and began to twirl. His mother asked, "What are you doing, sweetie?" He said, "I'm dancing with the angels."

This morning, I played guitar at church. After one set of worship songs, the congregation sat down. Mum kept standing. Her eyes were shut, and she was smiling, her face radiant.

I have no doubt that Mum too was dancing with the angels.

The tumor can't stay for the angels have made her whole, and now, the doctors scratching their heads and saying it's not discernible, that after the hurting and weeping and sleeping for days, the tumor has disappeared.

And while Mum is still missing part of her right frontal lobe, she is learning life again, life and laundry and laughter, and when I come to visit she asks about Aiden.

She remembers his name, and I kiss her for remembering. I kiss her rosy cheeks, and Mum smiles and knows it is a good day.

St. Joseph Island, Ont.
July 14, 1988

I don't easily get excited about "happy" events, partly because I've got used to being disappointed about something I'd been looking forward to and partly because usually there's lots of work involved with whatever project or festivity. . . . I've enjoyed camping by the beach. There hasn't been a lot of work and there's lots of free time for kids and me to do what we like to do. I've read three books this week and played with the kids—that's "exciting!"

I do get excited by beautiful, unexpected sights, and "free gifts," as it were, that I didn't have to work for. I get excited by the children's accomplishments—Emily's musical ability for example, Keith's insightful questioning, Allison's helpfulness and inquiring mind and Meredith's bubbly enthusiasm.

Music can excite me—"move" me emotionally; good hymns, worshipful singing, instrumentals.

37

Moving

Canada: Neerlandia, Alberta

April 2010

> The real voyage of discovery consists not in seeking new landscapes, but in having new eyes.
>
> Marcel Proust

Mum is at the door, laden with bags stuffed with books, slippers, diapers. It's Wednesday. She has been dropped off by one of the Coffee Break ladies, as she is every week; Dad has gone to his chaplaincy job at Wingham Hospital.

Aiden is crying from somewhere deep inside him, a cry I'm not sure how to soothe, so I just pat his bum and whisper prayers begging God to breathe quiet so I can tend to Mum.

Then, when my son finally rests, I turn, and she's sitting at the table, still in her winter coat and boots, smiling at me. Winter frosted on her cheeks. Slowly I help her thaw; we eat pea soup together, she tells me about her morning, pulls out her pills, and spends the next hour trying to swallow them.

I help her down for her nap, tucking her deep under the duvet, pulling the blinds, kissing her forehead, and praying God give her rest to heal her mind. Mum turns to me, touches my cheek. "I love you bigger than biggest," she says. Eyes like blue earthenware on the pillow. I nod, swallow hard, kiss her one more time. Shut the door.

I hear Jesus echoing Mum, from humble-hanging on the cross. Loving us bigger than biggest. Every hour, every day.

God's love for us often looks like suffering. It often looks like the silhouette of the cross, when in fact it is the sun beyond that silhouette, rising on the third day.

On another Wednesday, close to Easter, Mum's legs carry her on topply feet in noon light, all the way from the CRC church to my house, bearing her tote bag and her coffee mug, which she brings everywhere.

She arrives, a pearl of sweat on her lip, cheeks flushed. She arrives triumphant, having walked from Coffee Break to my house, when normally she is driven.

These are significant steps, since three years ago she lay curled on the couch for days at a time unable to move or walk. The tumor is shrinking. God is moving.

Staring now at my baby's legs leaping high in his jolly jumper, springing into the air like fleshy pogo sticks, drool-goatee on his chin, mouth wide with baby delight, I see my husband's dreams in him. The ones he denied so he could help me help my parents. I've promised him that one day we'll move; that one day we will live close to his parents—his father still having back trouble and needing help on the farm—so our children can know life on a farm too, and even as Mum's legs are moving I'm wondering if it's time for us to move, as well.

Alberta lives in my husband's eyes and I live to see him happy. Ontario has been good to us, Trent subbing in different schools and playing on squash teams and tennis teams and hockey teams, but when he talks about home he talks about the west. I've never known a man to love his family more and to respect his childhood more, and he wants to give his children the same.

Aiden is jumping and I picture him running across Alberta soil, hopping on the quad and riding far into fields of canola, racing up and down piles of dirt and then pausing by the cows, piling off the quad and running fingers through cows' coarse hair as they stand in silence and lick salt. I picture him floating boats down a pregnant creek in the springtime, then climbing into a tub and riding that same creek using old hockey sticks as paddles.

I can see the harvest, the air thick with chaff and the yellow of the canola rising to meet the blue of sky. The smell of exhaust from the tractor. Marge's Oh Henry squares and the Easter egg hunts and the sand hills, golden and round, and us sliding down them every fall and taking a picnic with us, across the river on the Vega ferry—the only free ferry in North America, the one Trent's grandpa used to run. I can picture the co-op with its Dutch licorice and aisles of groceries and its post office, the Christian public school across the road Trent attended kindergarten to grade ten, and the ice rink behind it that sells hot chocolate and its Friday Night Skates, where adults stand around the rim and chat while the children spin in the middle.

And the July 1 picnic, with its pancake breakfast and three-legged races and boot-throwing contest, with its barbecue lunch and baseball games and fireworks.

I picture snowmobiling in winter, ripping across the fields and pulling others on tubes and then mugs of cocoa and board games at the kitchen table and everyone is always welcome at Marge's house.

God is everywhere and everywhere is home if God is in it, but sometimes he also directs us to specific places.

And I know that for Trent, God feels closest out west, in the Dutch hamlet of Neerlandia, in the wide open skies and the dry heat and the call of the geese. And don't I live to help my family, my husband, my children; to know God more? To know love more?

And I wonder, is it time?

Mum's steps make me think it is. Time to pick up from our crowded home and move to the open fields where Trent can watch his son's legs grow and chase calves and run after stray kittens and play Canadian Cricket on his grandma's lawn.

It would be an act of faith, for still, no job, no house—so when is it faith? And when is it foolishness?

And I think of Jesus's legs cracked and bleeding on the Easter-cross and I see in him the foolishness of a weak God, then, three days later, legs strong and whole, standing in the garden before Mary and Thomas and the disciples telling the world to touch and see, he is God. And he is power. And he is trustworthy. In spite of appearing foolish and weak.

Begging God, then, today, to show me how to make wobbly steps in this walk of the Spirit. To know when to move and when to stand still.

Mum and Dad have given us their blessing, and Trent has an interview with his alma mater, Neerlandia Christian Public, and he tells me how, when he was young, his dream was to teach math at that school.

He's up against a few other candidates, and in spite of having a migraine and a sore throat the day of the interview, and doing it over Skype, he is offered the job of junior high math teacher.

And so, we move.

I hold on to Mum for a long time in the entrance of her home and Dad, right behind her, and I can't seem to let go.

But she is smiling and thanking me and saying I need to. I need to let my husband follow his dreams and Dad is hugging me now and thanking me for all of my help and telling me, "Godspeed."

We latch a trailer to our veggie car, full of blue plastic tubs, full of our possessions, and friends of ours taking another trailer out west for us too, going there anyway.

The veggie car breaks down in Saskatchewan; we've been filling it up at KFCs and other fast-food restaurants, and then one afternoon we stop for lunch at the side of the road, and when we try to start the car, it won't. It takes Trent an hour to get it going, and we are off in an enclosed area where no one can see us so there are a lot of desperate prayers.

When it finally starts, I slide behind the wheel and soon the car begins to swerve back and forth and the trailer is whipping the VW from side to side. At one point, we're in the wrong lane with an oncoming semi and the next, we're in the ditch and we look to the right and see the trailer passing us, upside down. Aiden squealing in the backseat like it's a ride at the carnival and my knuckles gripped white around the wheel.

The trailer keeps going, lands by a pond, our world spilling humpty-dumpty across the grass in blue tubs and cardboard boxes and I pick up Aiden, who knows no different, pick up the wedding photos splayed across the ditch and look at my husband, his face twisted. And we wait.

And they descend, the angels in a semi, a minivan, and a brand-new Honda, and they take us and make us hope. They put our trailer on a skid and send it to Saskatoon and take our bodies and put them in a motel and they take our car and put it in a shop, and they say, "You should have flipped."

We say thank you. It sounds much like a prayer.

Marge comes out in her van the next day, drives out with her sister, even as the car is being fixed at a local shop, and we stuff our belongings into her van and then drive slowly, the rest of the way home.

That is the end of the veggie car. It dies in the back of Harvey's farm, and we purchase a silver Subaru even as we live at Marge's for the next month, in a room in the back of her extended trailer, and pray that our house in Blyth will sell.

We have savings, and we can dip into them, but not for long.

Our plan is to rent out our Blyth house, because no one seems to be buying, and we've had dozens of renters applying and my dad, answering their phone calls and giving them tours. But we long to have it sold.

And even while we wait, we search the hamlet for a place to live. There are two mobiles for sale, and a newly renovated home with three bedrooms, a play room with a chalkboard built into the wall, a huge open kitchen with hardwood flooring and a walk-in pantry, a living room with a built-in entertainment center, and an office. Then, as we walk outside onto the covered deck, the residents say, "And this is where we watch the thunderstorms," and over to our right we see a fenced-in play area for the kids with a wooden playground and sandbox. And I know. This is it.

And then our house in Blyth sells, even as we sign the papers in Neerlandia.

And Mum's tumor continues to collapse. It's less than five millimeters, now, doctors unsure if it is even a tumor anymore.

Sometimes, for a split second, life's problems just sort of line up and solve themselves and you see the hand of Jehovah Jireh so gloriously and heavily. Just for a second. Like God shining on Moses's face and then he's gone, but still, the shine.

And for months afterward your face is alight.

We have Friday morning phone dates, Mum dialing, and sometimes it takes her three tries to punch in the right number, speaking soft into the receiver as it slips out of her hand and me, four thousand miles away, missing her.

My baby's walking now and he falls, pushes bum up and into the air and off again, while Mum's British accent wraps the receiver 'round.

We talk about what she did that day; drinking coffee with church ladies, nap time, what she's reading. We talk about baths, and how good they feel. About mochas, and how delicious they are. About the latest Karen Kingsbury book and the movies Mum's slept through and then, the hush of knowing we've talked enough and so begins the goodbye. And we whisper, mother-daughter-like, across the shaky miles.

Amidst the "I love you biggers," Mum says, "I want to show you just how much I love you." And I hear her lips press against the phone in a kiss and it is the sound of God's faithfulness to the generations. His long eternal arms wrapping us close across the miles.

We cannot be apart, so long as we are in him.

38

Tithing

Mexico: Cancun

March 2011

> As you simplify your life, the laws of the universe will be simpler; solitude will not be solitude, poverty will not be poverty, nor weakness, weakness.
>
> Henry David Thoreau

My womb is bulging again with a sibling for Aiden and we're flying to Mexico for a getaway. It's a vacation Trent bought me at Christmas, and we're using it during March Break.

We won a week at a resort in Cancun and I thought it would be easy to accept food from waiters and to tan on the beach, but all I can see are the poor beyond the gates.

It's a broken spirit, mine, shattered like blue glass across the beaches of Mexico.

"We all have stories," he tells us, the man in the suit, the one trying to sell us pipes on the beach, and he talks about growing up with six siblings and never going on vacation. The man next to us, selling coconuts, says his father was killed and he was left with nothing. The one who drinks too much and wears dark shades and laughs loud, he lost his six-year-old daughter to leukemia.

Women sell woven cloth in bright colors, the same colors they're wrapped in, on the sidewalks and around their waists. They make bracelets while beside them babies sleep in the grass and my heart winds tight and I want to see them at home in rocking chairs, feet up, babies tucked tight in blankets.

"What can we do?" I say to Trent.

Seashells, dozens, lined up outside homes that are metal-roofed shacks, tumbling down around the garbage and the dogs, and we buy some shells, feel as though we've helped but really? Now, to return to our clean floors and our stocked fridge and our air-conditioned elevators?

And the woman with the child twisted out of shape standing by the pier with a sign pleading for help and all we have are a banana and a box of fruit loops but we give and I touch this little boy's arm strapped in a shaft and whisper "Hola" into his eyes and he doesn't move but the mother starts telling me her story in Spanish and all I can do is sob into Trent's shirt.

There are shadows here in Mexico, in all of the hard places, in the space between humanity and hell, the jagged gaps between rich and poor, the brown skin grooves and the threads of color between their fingers.

And I fold my hands and bow my head and entreat the one who is light to come, Lord Jesus, come.

I am curled into a ball of prayer in a hidden place behind the restaurant after Trent tells me: we've made a big mistake. We'd spent $9,500 on a time share we would never use.

We'd told everyone that we'd never get suckered in. And we hadn't, until the final moments when they said the deal could be used worldwide, and the vacations could be in log cabins instead of resorts, and we thought it sounded like a perfect way to help our boys see the world, only we didn't read the fine print. And the champagne bottle popped and they told us to keep it quiet, for no one else had gotten the deal we have, and they upscaled our room and it felt pretty good, until the fine print.

The print Trent reads later in the restaurant. We've been misled. The deal we signed up for requires that we do all-inclusive every time. And we have already decided we can never do all-inclusive again. We don't want to raise our sons in such affluence, and all I can do is stare at the limp piece of lettuce on my plate.

They are famous for making it hard to cancel deals and so I run. I run behind the restaurant to a patch of grass and I cry and beg God to save us, for it has all been a mistake.

A gardener slips past me, and then it comes. God's voice. And he says, *I will restore everything to you. Every penny. But you must make me a promise. You must dedicate that money to me. Use it for my glory.*

Anything, Lord, I say. And I run to Trent, who's folded hands over knees, and I tell him what God has said and he believes and we bow in prayer together.

Two months later, with papers filed and contract canceled and Trent on the phone to Mexico and them saying yes, they'll return the money, but they'll keep the amount for the room we'd upscaled to, the room they'd given as a gift for the deal, and that was going to cost us thousands. And then Visa steps in to help us. Warns us it can take three to four months and still then, maybe we'll lose.

And one week later, when I'm out running errands, Trent calls me on the cell. "It's back," he says, hoarse. "The money. All of it. Back in our bank account."

We tuck all of that money into an account called "Blessings Fund" and the rule, Trent says, is if you feel like giving, then give.

"It's for the above and beyond gifts," he says. "In addition to our tithing."

The money has been returned, and yet it's God's. It's been returned and yet it was never ours in the first place.

The closer we let ourselves get to Jesus, the more we learn the way he sees. We learn the way he loves. And we learn the way he gives. And he never stops giving and we never stop receiving.

39

Laughter

Canada: Jasper and Canmore, Alberta

July 2011

> Life is worth living as long as there's a laugh in it.
>
> L. M. Montgomery

I wake to the smell of the forest, all spruce gum and rain-wet, to the sound of a bird's winded wing and the touch of a man curled into a boy as he sleeps on the air mattress beside me.

I wake to the blue of a tent made bright by the sun, to the way air was meant to be, all fresh and full and the warmth of a sleeping bag around my extended womb kicking with a newborn near-ready.

And some think me crazy to go camping in a tent in Jasper, at Snaring River, at thirty-nine weeks pregnant with our second son, but how to explain that it would have been death to stay home? To fail to remember what it's like to live before giving birth to new life? To bring another soul into a world I'd forgotten? To make a family in a space I felt folding up around me?

And so I had to escape to the mountains, to the bed beneath the stars, because it's so easy to forget what makes life tick when staring into the screen of a computer. So easy to think life consists of peering into the dustpan and the sink and the potty, to make existence a mere combination of hand and apron and foot, when it's all God.

And I find him in the campsite, in the flicker of a kerosene lantern, in the giggle of a boy picking up sticks and stones, in the charcoal edge of a pancake and the crispness of bacon and in a husband washing my feet in an enamel tub while cicadas sing and the red fire dances.

I find God in the melted s'mores and the watery Tang and the walks by turquoise water. In the slip of a wrist skipping stones, in the rise of a mountain, in the swing of an outhouse door and the sound of an axe cracking wood and the little boy asking "Da?" when a squirrel chatters.

For these are the moments in which we stare into the face of God, in which we feel his breath; these are the reasons we sweep up dust and potty-train and stare at the computer screen.

I'd been feeling scared. Scared of labor. Scared of becoming "just a mom" with two kids and no time to write. Scared of the hum of the dryer and the whir of the dishwasher and the toys scattered on the ground and all of it seeming meaningless.

I needed to get out. Out of my house, out of my chair—the tan one in the corner of the living room, where I write—out of my apron and my slippers and into the sanctuary that is God's breath. That is life, pulsing, that is the reminder that we are but dust and life is so much bigger than what we can see. It is all of our five senses and then some. It is the force of prayer that throws us to the ground in fear of the Creator who made all of this. Who made the Rockies and the boy in his baseball cap and the man in his sandals and us walking trails, seeking him. Our Father. Wanting to walk and talk with him and always seeking. It's in the seeking that we find the love that reminds us we are nothing and he is everything.

And we render ourselves helpless in order to give birth.

It is two weeks later and I've borne my eight-pound, fourteen-ounce Kasher Jude, in Barrhead, Alberta, after thirty-two hours of labor. A stocky boy with a hearty cry who God says is a courageous warrior. A boy whose name means "authentic praise."

And I've just found out my book has been rejected by the publisher that's been courting it for a year.

It's a book I've written about my eating disorder, and I'm very quiet on our family vacation. Trying to swallow the sadness. Trying to believe God has a plan for me that I just can't see. Trying to believe, again—all over again—that he wants to give us good gifts.

We're in Canmore and around us, the Rocky Mountains, the kinds one could run to and we've run together this August to a family holiday.

Mum in her new floral shirt and Dad in his "holiday" blue jeans and Keith with his family—Darcie and the two kids, Isaiah and Lucy; Allison; and Meredith with her husband, Davies; and Dad reading Bill Cosby out loud to us in the condo living room and he can't stop laughing.

His face is wrinkled with happiness.

Dad always lets go on vacations. He eats what he wants and makes puns and plays games, and when I was young I always looked forward to holidays and dreaded when they ended because Dad was fun on vacation. And life itself, growing up—the day to day, with all of its "must-dos"—didn't contain much joy.

Even so, it is new, this sort of laughing. Not a chuckle or a polite giggle but one that opens the soul wide, and I used to push all of my father's buttons in hopes of him showing some feeling. And now he finally is.

Dad is being moved to joy because of grandchildren and Mum's recovery and realizing church is more than a building. And he's trusting us enough to express his emotions around us. To stop guarding his heart and to start letting life sing to him. To be vulnerable, and it's only in being vulnerable that we can be fully loved.

I slip inside to nurse Kasher, and I think about how easy it would be to keep one's children from feeling, for the agony it causes. Sometimes when Aiden cries I offer him a cookie, but isn't that just using food to cram down the emotion, and isn't that what an eating disorder does?

I need to learn to let him cry, to hold him while he does. To not tell him "It's okay" when for him it isn't. When for him it is the end of the world. All I wanted when I was little and starving was for my dad to come into my bedroom and hold me. To pick me up and tell me he was sorry, and to hold me, to sit with me in the darkness of my eating disorder. But fear can keep us from extending love.

And I promise myself, even as I watch Kasher's cheeks expand and deflate, my body feeding him, to just let my boys sit in tears for a little while. To feel the sadness with them. And maybe suffering on behalf of another is the greatest gift of all, because it offers a kind of love that sacrifices. That sees beyond today.

This, the hardest thing for a parent to do. To not fix. To just let. For then we have to trust God to do the healing, while we simply hold.

But in the end I know my children are worth the feeling, that they are worth this moment, and that love is real in a painful kind of way, the kind that makes a person double over, the kind that puts a Savior on a cross.

We are home now from the mountains, and it's been a week since I've seen Mum.

It's Friday, and I'm sitting on the rocking chair Trent brought outside for me, in a patch of sun, the chair my grandmother used to rock on, and I'm sitting in my apron and chatting with Mum on the phone.

I'm telling her about her smile, about the way I can't stop thinking about it—and how could she smile so often, having gone through what she had?

There is silence and then, "I didn't used to, you know," Mum says. "Smile."

"What do you mean?"

"Before I got married . . . before university . . ."

I wait. Aiden's riding his tricycle in circles around the chair.

"Before I met Jesus," Mum says slowly. "He's the reason I smile. It's all him."

Soon we say goodbye, and I head into the house and pull loaves from the oven and Aiden is sitting on top of the counter like he always does. And he's so hungry he just tears off the crust from one of the loaves and starts eating.

And I let him, because it fills him.

When he is full, he smiles, and I realize, a smile is the overflow of needing nothing else.

The spilling of crumbs from lips to world.

40

See How Much I Love You

Canada: Neerlandia, Alberta

> I love you without knowing how, or when, or from where. I love you simply, without problems or pride: I love you in this way because I do not know any other way of loving but this, in which there is no I or you, so intimate that your hand upon my chest is my hand, so intimate that when I fall asleep your eyes close.
>
> Pablo Neruda

There is a certain kind of graciousness to love.

When the light strikes I see us fifty years from now, happy, grey, grooved, wearing dentures, my dress on backward and my lipstick on crooked and happy.

That light finds me worn on a day so awful, a day when the dishwasher crusts dirt onto glass, a day when the car won't start because the battery died when I forgot to shut the door after Aiden burned his hand on the woodstove.

Burned his hand.

A day when there seems no redemption, but it comes in the stumble of an eight-year-old marriage, a marriage graduating kindergarten, a marriage learning to share and do its homework and to play together at recess.

"I was thinking this morning," Trent stammers, as I cry over crusted dishes.

"I was thinking . . ."

And I'm barely listening for the grime.

"How much I love you. I really do."

Then he steps outside and shuts the door and I finally hear him.

And I don't need to cry anymore. All I need is to fill the sink with suds and scrub the glass clean because he loves me.

The light slants fifty-year-old rays, across our sons' faces.

Warming them like the love of the ages.

I lie in red pajamas on the living room sofa, and Trent, on the other in his comfy clothes, in his green ribbed shirt with the hole and his fuzzy pants that have no waist and, "Our good times were more than our bad," he says in a voice that aches.

"Yes, but our bad times were so bad."

"But we never went to bed angry," says Trent. "We never stopped holding each other. Even on the worst nights, when you couldn't sleep, we would still watch shows together until finally you fell asleep in my arms. We ate pizza together, and I made you wings."

"That was my one meal of the day," I say. "I guess I was so focused on making it to that meal that I didn't notice the rest."

"But there was the other," says Trent. "There was always the other. We never had a fight we couldn't fix. I don't even remember what we were fighting about. We had, maybe, four big fights, but the rest of the time, it was good. And we never stopped holding each other. Never."

I stare at Trent's profile in the dark, the children asleep. I was sharp with him earlier that day. I'd swung at him with my voice, and it has quieted him.

Reminding him of the years when I wasn't eating, the years when hope felt skinny between us.

And Trent doesn't normally talk about those years, but tonight, words find him and I listen as he wonders, "Why?"

Why had I done that to myself? To us? To him?

And I see the lines in his face. I see the nights in which I never came to bed. I see the days I refused to eat, colored grey beneath his eyes, and the afternoon I tried to drive us into traffic.

I can't tell him "I'm sorry" enough, and then I ask him, "How can you love me? After all of that?"

And Trent turns to me and the moon puddles in his eyes. And he reminds me, again, of what he's said before.

"I love all of you. For better or for worse. And no matter what happens, that will never change."

He doesn't say much, but what he does say matters, and at night we visit the garden because these are the things Trent says are important.

"Let's hold hands and walk each row and see how things are growing," he says, and we are both in our pajamas and we touch palms along the dirt path.

He puts me in the moment, so that I really taste the watermelon and see the way the light makes green our sons' eyes, the way the wind moves the trees' leaves and how the mourning dove sings outside our window.

And as we walk, we leave behind the skinny years, the hard years, turning them into the forgotten years, and Trent holds my heart as he holds my hand, and whispers into my ears even as it is scribbled across the sky: how much I am fully alive, fully here, fully loved.

Epilogue

It's been three years since we walked those furrowed rows, and our boys are four and a half and three now. We lost another child last year, at eight weeks, and it was hard. We called her Madeleine, and we planted a tree for her.

We're loving our boys and watching them grow tall toward God. We tell them every day how much we love them and how they are kind and handsome, and we pray away the scary dreams at night and hold them close the day through.

Two years ago we fostered two boys for eleven months, and they still visit us every few weekends, and they are like my sons.

Trent is teaching nearly full-time now, with a permanent contract at Neerlandia Christian Public School, and I am writing books. My book on eating disorders was finally picked up by a small family publisher, and I cowrote another one with a doctor for mothers who long to know they're beautiful. I speak at conferences and churches, telling them my story of pain and redemption, and when time allows I paint and play guitar.

We continue to garden and we attend a small, faithful church, and Mum is well. So very well. She still has support workers come to help her grow her brain and relearn things like cooking and cleaning, and everything is slower for her now, but the tumor is gone and she hasn't slept through a Sunday in years. Dad is a happy grandfather of eight and all of us kids are married now.

And I'm learning every day how loved and lovely I am, only because of Jesus and what he sees in me, and I'm falling ever more in love with the man who got a tattoo with me for our tenth anniversary last year.

We got the Korean symbol 한, for han ("one body or flesh"), but it means more than that. Han is the sorrow and lamenting of times past. The example offered to explain the word is when a woman sees her lover off to war: she is sorrowful for his departure, but only because of the deep love that they share, for which she is grateful. It's the human condition, being aware that things are temporary.

The root of the word *han* comes from the Chinese character 恨, which is composed of two radicals: the one on the left is "heart" and the one on the right is "step." You can hear the sound of *han* in the voice of traditional Korean and Chinese singers, and it sounds very much on the verge of tears, like a sorrowful cry of nostalgia for times past.

Our marriage has not been a bed of roses but rather a friendship that has persevered. It has been the *hana* of relationships, the kind that endures triumphs and suffering.

And we held hands the day we got inked. We sat there in that tattoo parlor and went through pain, together, because in the end, the needle of suffering sketches the most beautiful picture.

A picture of joy.

Time Line

1980—Emily is born in Guelph, Ontario, to Ernest and Yvonne Dow

1981—Emily travels with parents to Nigeria and Congo, Africa, with the Christian Blind Mission

1982—brother Keith is born in Congo; family returns home to Mitchell, Ontario, Canada

1984—sister Allison is born; move from Mitchell to Staffa

1986—sister Meredith is born; Yvonne homeschools all four children and Ernest becomes an ordained minister

1986–1987—move from Staffa to Norwich to Richard's Landing, Ontario

1989—Ernest is pastor at the United Church in Richard's Landing; Emily starts to manifest signs of anorexia; doctors encourage parents to put her in school

1991—Emily is admitted into the SickKids hospital in Toronto for one week in an attempt to inspire recovery

1993—travel to California on a camping trip with family; Emily lives with her grandparents for a month and when she returns, her parents admit her into the general hospital because she is sixty pounds at five foot four; Emily begins to eat and recover

1994—move from Richard's Landing to Laird

1996—Emily goes on a mission trip to Atlanta, Georgia, to the Summer Olympics, and receives her sweet sixteen kiss

1998—Emily travels west to Edmonton, Alberta, to attend a one-year discipleship program at Mount Carmel Bible School, where she meets Trenton Wierenga

1999—Emily's Nanny commits suicide; Ernest and Yvonne and family move from Laird to Blyth, Ontario

2000—Trent and Emily break up; Emily attends The King's University College in Edmonton

2002—Trent and Emily get back together and become engaged; Emily graduates with a bachelor of arts degree in English and travels to Lebanon and Jordan for six months in the fall while Trent finishes up his bachelor of education degree at the University of Alberta

2003—Emily returns home and begins to restrict again; Yvonne contracts brain cancer and has her right frontal lobe removed; in July, Emily and Trent get married and go on a three-week honeymoon to the Maritimes

2003–2006—Emily continues to restrict while working as associate editor of *Living Light News*, and mentoring girls through Young Life; Trent serves as staff with Young Life

2006—Trent gives Emily an ultimatum in the spring, and she begins to eat again; that summer they sell their house and move to Wonju, Korea

2006–2007—Trent and Emily live in Asia and teach English, traveling to Japan, China, and Thailand

2007—in May, Emily moves home to take care of her Mum, who is very sick with brain cancer; she buys a house for her and Trent in her parents' hometown, and travels to Australia that November to visit her sister Allison

2007–2010—Emily freelances and takes care of her Mum while Trent serves as a substitute teacher

2008—Emily is hired as staff writer for a church newspaper; she conceives in Richmond, Virginia, and then miscarries at five weeks

2009—Emily conceives in New York City, travels first to the Dominican Republic during March Break, and then to Lake Como, Italy, for a writer's conference, and gives birth to Aiden Grey on November 12

2010—doctors tell Yvonne that her tumor has shrunk, and Emily and Trent move to Neerlandia, Alberta, to be close to Trent's parents

2011—Emily and Trent travel to Mexico during March Break; Emily gives birth to Kasher Jude on July 25, and vacations with her family in Canmore, Alberta, two weeks later

Acknowledgments

I started this book as a blog when I returned home from Korea to care for my mum in 2007.

The blog was a means of survival, of processing. It was only when a former English professor of mine, Dr. Carol Everest (one of my five readers), suggested I compile my posts into a book that I began to wonder if the Lord wanted me to share Mum's story with the world.

For a few years I put it aside, while a couple of my other books were published. Yet when Baker Books editor Jon Wilcox approached my agent, Sandra Bishop of MacGregor Literary, and asked if I would be interested in writing a travel memoir, I dusted off the archives and began to rewrite what had originally been titled "Mum's Dance."

So I want to thank Dr. Carol Everest for planting the seed, and for giving me a vision.

I want to thank my agent and friend, Sandra Bishop, for always believing in my relationship with my mum and in this book, even in its infancy.

I want to thank my editor Jon Wilcox for his initial request for the memoir, and for his tireless energy, applause, and prayers, not to mention insightful editing, without which this book could not have been.

To Baker's beautiful team for its intuition, dedication, heart for God, prayers, and marketing skills, including Ruth Anderson,

Lauren Carlson, Alicia Sheppard, Brianna DeWitt, Lindsey Spoolstra, Elizabeth Kool, Lanette Haskins, and Twila Bennett. I am so blessed to be part of such a sacred gathering.

Thank you to the generous and kind Mick Silva for his constant encouragement and early reading of the manuscript, for his grace and devotion of time.

To my friends Amanda Batty, Melanie Brasher, and Stephanie Christensen, who read and cheered me onward: I love you.

And thank you to all of you who offered to read the book and endorse it—you gave my words wings. Bless you.

I want to thank my family, extended and intimate, for having arms that stretch wide across the miles and faces that shine from having seen the glory of God. Thank you for grace, as we worked through the awkwardness, for hours spent editing and praying and communicating. Thank you for being so humble as to share your story with the world.

I want to thank my husband, Trenton Wierenga, whom I continue to fall madly in love with, for giving me up evening after evening as I worked on this manuscript, and for editing it with such gentleness when it was finished.

And to my two beautiful boys, Aiden Grey and Kasher Jude, who let Mommy write during quiet time and naptime: your lives are my greatest endorsement.

Finally, I want to thank my Abba Father whose delight in me is the one thing I live for, and the sole reason I write. I am yours.

Discussion Guide

Session 1

1. Why does Emily refuse to sit near the bus driver? How does this set the tone of the book? (chap. 2)
2. Why does Emily stop talking in Congo, and how does this parallel her decision to stop eating years later when she is confronted with similar feelings of confusion and heartache? (chap. 3)
3. How are Sundays woven into the book, and what do they symbolize? How are they viewed by Emily as a child, and by her Mum, when her Mum is battling cancer? (chap. 27)
4. How does Emily's view of Sundays and all that they represent change as she witnesses her father's relationship with his family developing? (chap. 27)
5. The book opens and closes describing Emily's relationship with her Mum. Why do you think this is? What is she trying to say about her spiritual journey? How did traveling around the globe looking for God lead her back home, and what does this say about the role God can play within the family unit? (chaps. 1, 36, and 37)

Session 2

1. What role does motherhood play in the book, and how does Emily's relationship to the concept of motherhood develop

as she learns to forgive and embrace her own upbringing? Additionally, what does the birthing of Emily's first son symbolize, in regard to her relationship with God and with her own family? (chap. 35)

2. Why does Emily initially think she cannot marry Trenton, and how does their separation prepare them for the trials that lie ahead? (chap. 10)
3. God is continually telling Emily, *Watch me take care of you.* How is this statement reflective of God's relationship to all of us? How does he show Emily his care, as she learns the extent of his Father-love? (chaps. 16, 20, and 33)
4. How is Emily's perception of her heavenly Father affected by her relationship with her biological father, and how does this change as she gets older? (chaps. 2, 4, and 7)
5. What is the vision Emily receives while in Lebanon, of her and the branch of a tree, and how is it prophetic of the next few years of her life? (chap. 13)

Session 3

1. What are the reasons Emily falls back into an eating disorder following her trip to the Middle East, and how does physical hunger become a substitute for spiritual hunger? (chaps. 15 and 22)
2. What ultimatum does Trent give Emily, and how does Emily's decision to choose love open up the door to true healing? (chap. 23)
3. What happened in Korea to make Emily realize she needed to go home, and why was it necessary for her to start eating and caring for herself before she could go home and take care of her Mum? (chap. 24)
4. What does Emily's Mum do whenever she hears music or worship songs, and how does this represent healing from

her childhood, and the ballet classes she used to take? (chap. 9)

5. What memory does Yvonne have of her and Ernest, when they were young and in love? How has brain cancer rekindled romance between them, thereby healing Emily? (chap. 28)

Session 4

1. What role does prophecy play in the book, and what forms does it take, particularly in regard to Emily's future career, her and Trent's reunification, and their children? (chap. 11)
2. At what point does Emily begin to consider moving back out west, and how does Easter play a role in this decision? (chap. 37)
3. Why does Emily blame herself for her mother's tumor, and how does she eventually learn to forgive herself and her maternal grandmother, in regard to her Nanny's suicide? (chaps. 8 and 9)
4. How does Emily's blowup at Stan, her Bible school principal, represent the suppressed feelings she has toward her own father and authority figures in general? (chap. 7)
5. How is Emily's determination not to let her brother get hurt again juxtaposed with her decision to starve herself years later? (chap. 2)

Session 5

1. How does Emily's father's breaking down and finally asking for help result in healing? (chap. 25)
2. What is the purpose of including Yvonne's journal entries in the book, and what picture do they paint of the woman who wrote them? (chap. 25)

3. What is the miracle that Emily encounters, Christmas of 2007? (chap. 30)
4. When does Emily realize how badly she wants a baby, and what song provides consolation for her as she grieves? (chap. 31)
5. What does the acronym SHMILY mean in the book? How do Emily and Trent speak it to each other, and when and how does God speak it to Emily? (chaps. 24 and 40)

Emily T. Wierenga is an award-winning journalist, columnist, artist, author, and blogger at www.emilywierenga.com. Her work has appeared in many publications, including *Prodigal Magazine*, *A Deeper Story*, *Christianity Today*, *The Better Mom*, *MOPS*, *Adbusters*, *Geez Magazine*, *The MOB Society*, Dayspring's *(in) courage*, and *Focus on the Family*. She speaks regularly about her journey with anorexia. She lives in Alberta, Canada, with her husband, Trenton, and their two sons.

COME VISIT
WITH AUTHOR
AND ARTIST
emily
wierenga
AT
EMILYWIERENGA.COM